All Change!

All Change!

Romani Studies through Romani eyes

Edited by Damian Le Bas and Thomas Acton

University of Hertfordshire Press

First published in Great Britain in 2010 by
University of Hertfordshire Press
College Lane
Hatfield
Hertfordshire
AL10 9AB

British Library Cataloguing in Publication Data
A catalogue record for this book is available from the
British Library

ISBN 978-1-905313-78-5

Design by Heavens and Earth Art
Printed in Great Britain by MPG Books Group,
Bodmin and King's Lynn

I am the common Rom

Gregory Dufunia Kwiek

Hello, I'm the common Rom.
When us Rom are organized and live in one area, that place is a *lageri*[1]

Hello, I'm the common Rom.
Some fool told me to reveal to *gadjé* that I'm a Rom, and stand up –
(I don't think this guy was a Rom).

Hello, I'm the common Rom.
What do you mean, we are trash, the lowest of the low?
Then we probably deserve the way *gadjé* treat us.

Hello, I'm the common Rom.
How dare you say my *vitsa*[2] were once slaves?
Maybe yours were, but certainly not mine.
Maybe those slaves were the really *trashy* Gypsies.

Hello, I'm the common Rom.
Who's from India, you mad man?

Hello, I'm the common Rom.
Education? Are you joking?
We can't change – it's in our blood.
We will always be stupid Rom.

Hello, I'm the common Rom.
What do you mean, "listen to the *magerdo*[3] *gadjo*"?
Get out of my face!

Hello, I'm the common Rom.
Bow your head when the *gadjo* passes,
don't get him angry,
don't speak Romanes or he will recognise us.

Hello, I'm the common Rom.
What do you mean *sue*?
I just want to get out of this mess.
I'll leave this town without looking back.

Hello, I'm the common Rom.
Again they recognised us as Rom!
I told you kids not to speak Romanes in front of the *gadjé*.
Now it's time to move again.
And why did you go and wear a long skirt, girl?
The *gadjo* knew right away we were Rom;
now we'll never get an apartment.

[1] concentration camp [2] clan [3] unclean

Contents

Editor's preface

Damian Le Bas

When Thomas Acton and Jane Housham of the University of Hertfordshire Press invited me to edit this volume, I was sure the task would be insurmountable: as difficult as providing accurate figures for the number of Romanies resident in the UK.

I was right. Without Jane's Olympian patience and the sterling editorial help given to me by Thomas, whose hand-drawn Romani books I read and was inspired by as a boy, this volume would never have seen the light of day.

I would like to extend my thanks to my fellow contributors: Ian, Adrian, Brian, Valdemar, Janet and Wayne; and also to those who attended the seminar at the University of Greenwich that gave birth to this book and who asked very thought-provoking questions. Without them this book would not have been possible. It has been a privilege to have remained in touch with them since. My final thanks go to Professor Acton for organising the seminar in the first place, to Dufunia Kwiek for chairing proceedings in good spirit, and to Jane Housham for believing in this book from its inception.

Final responsibility for any errors to be found in the text below lands, of course, at the door of my trailer. I cannot, however, guarantee that I will be there, should you come knocking.

Damian Le Bas
London, August 2009

Introduction: a new turning point in the debates over the history and origins of Roma/Gypsies/Travellers

Professor Thomas Acton

University of Greenwich

In 1992 a consensus on Romani history seemed to have been reached, in Western European scholarship at least, with the publication of the late Sir Angus Fraser's *The Gypsies*, a magisterial work embodying a century of research. And yet, by the turn of the century its narrative was under attack from all sides. Radical social-constructionist critics (such as Wim Willems in his *In Search of the True Gypsy: from Enlightenment to Final Solution*) argued that this Fraserian history was merely a projection of the non-Gypsy racialisation of Gypsies in the eighteenth century. Some Gypsy/Roma/Traveller intellectuals have used Willems' theory to insist that historical accounts must be rooted foremost in the varied accounts their communities give of themselves now.

On the other hand, those Gypsy/Roma/Traveller intellectuals committed to the Romani language and its Indian roots nonetheless insist that any account of how that language came to be in Europe, the Americas and indeed all over the world cannot simply dismiss it as a 'mystery', and still less the result of any primordial disposition to nomadism. It has to make sense in terms of plausible actions taken by real human beings. And as the Soviet Union crumbled, a new Romani intelligentsia emerged, cobbled together from the old apparatchiks of the East and the autodidact activists of the West, which simply did not fit into the range of possibilities envisaged by the old narratives. Nonetheless, this new leadership, subject to much critical self-scrutiny, and perhaps reluctant admiration, tempered by fear of community betrayal, wanted to claim historical legitimacy for themselves.

So, why should the Fraserian consensus, so long in the making and so dominant after publication, have been followed by such a lively period of historical revisionism? The answer surely lies in this emergence of a Gypsy/Roma/Traveller academic and intellectual community, asking new questions and presenting new critical challenges, because for them this identity was not something exotic but their own. The Romany and Traveller Family History Society in the UK currently has over 600 members. Forty years ago the embryonic 'Gypsy Education Movement' in England thought that history was the last thing Gypsy children needed to study. Now we realise that only by studying history can we actually confront its legacies of oppression, genocide and bitterness.

This is why in June 2008 the Department for Children, Schools and Families sponsored the first national Gypsy/Roma/Traveller History Month. The University of Greenwich and the Greenwich Traveller Education Service were delighted to offer a platform for these new currents of Gypsy/Roma/Traveller historical thought. All were welcome. It just so happens that all the platform speakers, and all the contributors to this volume apart from myself, were of Gypsy/Roma/Traveller heritage. The day was tightly chaired by the distinguished Romani poet and educator, Gregory 'Dufunia' Kwiek. As we studied the debates about the academic and theoretical history that lies behind the school history lessons, we were, in a small way, making history ourselves.

September 2009

Mind the doors!
The contribution of linguistics

Professor Ian Hancock

The Romani Archives and Documentation Center
The University of Texas at Austin

'The Gipseys are an eastern people, and have eastern notions.'
Grellmann, 1783: xj

For a very long time, the explanation of the circumstances leading to the departure of our ancestors from India seems to have been settled and the doors closed on that part of our history. They were, according to almost every popular source, the 10,000 or 12,000 musicians who were sent as a gift from India to Persia in the middle of the fifth century. The list of accounts of this is a long one but I will give a couple of examples from the past few years. Telerama released a film entitled *Rom* in 1990 where this story was presented as unequivocal fact. Soon after that, Harcourt Films released its own documentary entitled *The Romany Trail* in which this same history was recounted accompanied by animated maps, once again the exodus from India being explained by referring to Firdausi's *Shah Nameh*. The story has now wandered its way into *The Encyclopedia of Multicultural America*, although here both the date and the number differ widely and a new name and reference to 'linguistic evidence' is introduced:

> Near the end of the ninth century B.C. an Indian King, Shangul, sent 1,000 *Dom* to Persia (now Iran) as minstrel musicians ... linguistic evidence indicates that after a hundred years or so of entertaining Persians in the tenth century, the *Dom* began to roam far afield. They separated into two major groups and lived as nomads. The first group

to leave wandered into Syria … the second group traveled northward from Persia into Armenia [and] after passing through Byzantine Greece, the Northerners reached Eastern Europe (Heimlich, 1994: 627–8).

Tony Gatlif's beautiful film *Latcho Drom*, which appeared in 1993, presented the same historical scenario, as did Marlene Sway in her book *Familiar Strangers: Gypsy Life in America* (1988) and Elizabeth Sirimarco in her *Endangered Cultures: Gypsies* (2000). The entertainer connection is supported by Matras (1999: 1), who says that 'Indic diaspora languages [are] spoken by what appear to be descendants of itinerant castes of artisans and entertainers who are spread throughout Central Asia, the Near East and Europe. They include … Romani,' and more recently by Tcherenkov and Laederich (2004). They say:

> [It] is but a small step to support the hypothesis that the[se] Indian *Dom* are the ancestors of the European Rroma. The professions exercised by the *Dom* in the Indian subcontinent – musicians, dancers, smiths, basket weavers, sieve makers, even woodworkers, are transmitted from father to son. From their similarity to the ones of the European Rroma these could or may be considered as the origins of the traditional Rroma trades.

But the social, historical and linguistic evidence now available to us has demanded that those closed doors be opened and the details of our origins be examined anew.

Paspati's statement that the history of our people must be sought in our language has become something of a cliché in Romani studies, but to a great extent it holds true. However, the assumption implicit in the scholarship of the eighteenth and nineteenth centuries that there was a connection between one's genetic history and the specific language one speaks has long been recognised as false, and that fact must temper our interpretation of the linguistic data. I remind my students that there are those among their classmates of German, Czech, African, Asian and Native American ancestry, but that they are all native speakers of English. The study of our language is intimately bound up with our identity. I want to deal with both aspects, but will talk about language first.

Westerners have been aware of the Romani language for as long as our people have been among them, but they were not able to identify it, or us, until several centuries had gone by. Some of the early Romanies did in fact tell the Europeans where they'd come from: Foroliviensis, for example, reported that the Romanies he met in Italy in 1422 'said they were from India' (Muratori, 1754) and a Spanish rabbi wrote about a similar encounter in the same century. Even earlier, it was probably Romanies the Irish friar Simon Fitzsimons met when he visited the lands around the eastern Mediterranean between 1322 and 1324, subsequently writing about the 'Indians' there, 'all of whom have much in common with crows and charcoal'. He also referred to their military involvement when he reported that they were 'always at war … with the Danubians' (Hoade, 1952: 10–11, 36, and see especially Piasere [1988] for further discussion). Sebastian Münster reported in 1544 that he had understood from a conversation with some Roma in Germany that their home was 'in Asia, along the Ganges or the Indus'. Cesare Vecellio too had written about an Indian origin for the Roma in 1590, placing their home in Calcutta. Liégeois tells us that *Indiens* was a name applied to Romanies in a document from France dated 1632 (Piasere, 1988). But even though we have references to an Indian identity which date from the Middle Ages, the concept of 'India' itself meant little to the medieval European peasantry, and in time the connection became lost and was replaced by several others, some of them highly imaginative: an origin on the Moon, from inside the hollow earth, from Atlantis, from among the Jews, the Nubians, the Scythians and so on. This confusion with other, non-Romani populations blurred distinctions and reinforced the idea that 'gypsies' were a composite population of native origin, defined by behaviour and not by history or place. It has been precisely this vagueness regarding Romani identity that has allowed the ease of its manipulation by outsiders, a point I have made several times. But this manipulation has also been helped by the conflicting notions of identity that exist within the different Romani populations themselves, and there's a reason for that too.

The conventional account of the establishment of the Indian linguistic connection involves one Vályi István, a student at Leiden University who in the early 1760s reportedly overheard three students from Malabar in south-western India discussing their native language, and who recognised similarities with the Romani he had picked up from the labourers on his family's estate. According to Samuel ab Hortis, author of the first of several accounts of this episode, Vályi obtained a list of over a thousand words from those Indian students, the meanings of *all* of which he said the Romanies knew 'without any problems or difficulty'.

This account finally got into print in 1776 and set the stage for the emergence of Romani studies. When I went to the University of Leiden in 1990 to investigate for myself, however, I found *no* record of Vályi's ever having been a student there, but discovered instead that he had attended the University of Utrecht a decade earlier. It seems likelier that someone else – perhaps Horvath, perhaps Bacmeister, Bryant or Rüdiger – was responsible for this historic breakthrough (Hancock, 1992). But not only has the list he was supposed to have compiled never been found, Romani is in any case quite unrelated to the Dravidian language of Malabar, and has two or three hundred Indian roots fewer than the more than one thousand words on Vályi's list even if they *had* been collected in a related Indian language. Regardless, the assumption was that if the Romanies spoke a language from India, then they must be from India themselves, which brings me back to my earlier cautionary statement. This was a cavalier supposition, although it happened to be true, at least in part. Grellmann (1783), like Tcherenkov and Laederich whom I quoted from just now, seeing the low and marginalised social and occupational status of Romanies in Europe, concluded that this simply reflected a continuation of their original position within Indian society. He identified the *Zigeuner* with the *Śudras* – he called them *Suders* – members of the lowest of the four Hindu castes. Later, in 1841, a man named Hermann Brockhaus suggested that the word *Rom* had its origin in the Indian word *dom*, which refers to a class of people which the dictionary describes as '…a very low caste, representing some old aboriginal race, spread all over India. They perform such offices as carrying dead bodies, removing carrion, and so on'. Sinclair (1909: 40) defines them even less charitably as being 'the very dregs of impurity, the Helots of all, shameless vagrants, eaters of carrion, beggars and thieves'. Very quickly, this origin became the conventional wisdom in Romani studies, and is repeated even today without qualification in books about Romanies. Matras (2004: 278), for example, has recently written that:

> Proto-Romani was carried from India westwards by migrants who appear to have been members of service-providing castes, similar in status and occupational profile to jatis or service groups known in some parts of India as dom … the řom settled in the Byzantine Empire some time around the tenth century CE.

In the early nineteenth century, the existence of two more apparently Indian languages spoken outside of India became known; these were Lomavren and Domari. Lomavren, spoken in Armenia, Georgia, eastern Turkey and probably elsewhere in the region, was first brought to the attention of European scholars in 1828 when a list of 100 words was published by von Joakimov (mentioned in Finck, 1907: 2). The first published account of Domari was by Pott (1844–5), in which he summarised notes on the language sent to him by the Reverend Eli Smith, an American missionary who had worked in Syria in the early 1800s. By the end of that century, John Sampson had constructed his well-known hypothesis, which saw a single migration leaving India in the ninth century that moved through Persia and then separated into three branches: the Domari speakers or Dom remaining in the Middle East, the Lomavren speakers or Lom moving off into Armenia, and the Romani speakers or Rom continuing on westwards and eventually coming into Europe.

Shared Indian linguistic similarities persuaded Sampson to see a common origin for Romani and Domari:

> It may be inquired whether the language of the Asiatic and that of the European Gypsies had a common origin, or whether the two forms of speech are so distinct as to warrant us supposing that they may have belonged to separate Indian peoples living perhaps under different conditions of time and place. To this question there can be but one answer. In spite of the outward dissimilarity between the Eastern and the Western Romani of to-day, an analysis of their grammar, the true criterion of relationship, makes it clear that both languages were originally one … thus finally establishing the close relationship of the two dialects despite their long separation (1923: 160).

He believed that 'Gypsies, on first entering Persian territory, were a single race speaking a single language … separation [into Romani and Domari] could only have taken place after their arrival in Persia'. And that his work 'proves conclusively that both languages spring from a single source, which must have been the parent speech of the Gypsies when they first entered Persian territory' (1926: 34). But Adrian Colocci (1907: 279) urged caution in drawing too sweeping a conclusion from the available data:

> To imagine that just because the Gypsies of Europe and their brothers in Asia share a common linguistic core, one should therefore conclude that there was a single exodus of these people [out of India], and furthermore that the unity of their language argues against more than one migration, seems to be a conclusion which is only slightly weakened by the still nebulous state of the documentation.

> Unity of language might well prove unity of origin; but there could still have been different migrations, chronologically and geographically, without that fact being too apparent from the lexical adoptions acquired by the mother tongue in the countries through which they passed; all the more so since those migrations were very rapid.

> To conclude, therefore, that the unity of their exodus rests upon the recognition of the unity of the substrate of their language, strikes

me as a proposition which shouldn't be universally accepted without [first incorporating] the benefit of a [lexical] inventory.

Turner (1927: 176) agreed with Colocci, and wrote that:

[T]he morphological differences between European and Syrian Romani [i.e. Domari] are very considerable, and many of the resemblances can be referred back to a common Indian *origin* rather than necessarily to a post-Indian period of *community*.

He was saying, in other words, that while Romani and Domari are both Indic, this does not necessarily mean that the ancestors of both constituted one population while they were still in India. Gypsy Lore Society member A.C. Woolner also wrote in a letter to Dora Yates dated 21 September 1932 that he was 'not convinced that the origin of Syrian Romani (*sic*) and European Romani are the same'.

Nevertheless it is *still* widely accepted that the Dom, Lom and Rom branches of Gypsy are related in terms of their original speakers having left India as one population, separating only once they had passed through Persia. In 1972 Walter Starkie brought all of the ideas current in his day together in one statement:

[Gypsies] are still as mysterious as when they entered Europe in the fifteenth century. Sprung from Dravidian stock in the northwest of India, they were pariahs, and according to tradition metal-workers, minstrels, story-tellers and fakirs. They spoke a language which was derived from Sanskrit, and we find them mentioned in the *Shah Nameh*, or *Book of the Kings*, by Persia's most famous poet, Firdausi (935–1020), who calls them *Luris*, the name by which they are known today in Iran. From Persia the Gypsies wandered on to Armenia, and from there into Syria and the Byzantine Empire.

It is upon the basis of such pronouncements by non-specialist academics and authors writing far outside of their area of expertise that erroneous perceptions of history pass into the popular domain.

Determining the relationship of Lomavren is not quite so straightforward, since its Indian link survives only in its vocabulary. In light of the koine hypothesis it may in fact have only ever existed as a Para-Romani language. Nevertheless, some years before Turner voiced his suspicions that Domari had a different linguistic history from Romani, Finck (1907: 49–50) had also made the same claim for Lomavren, which he believed was probably of Indic (Śaurasenī) descent, unlike Romani, which he saw as a Dardic language. Nevertheless, it is Sampson's position that has become the established one; all attempts to describe Proto-Gypsy have assumed it. Kaufman (1984) called his protoform *Dōmbari*, and called its speakers *dōmba*, while Tálos (1999) preferred the name *Dommānī*. Higgie called it Proto-Romani. Kaufman's reconstruction utilised items found in each of Romani, Domari and Lomavren; such reconstructed forms have, therefore, incorporated phonological changes found in all three. This would be rather like including Gothic in a reconstruction of Proto-Low West Germanic.

To his credit, Sampson (1923: 164) admitted that 'lacking in Nuri [that is, Domari] are several important loanwords [from Persian occurring in Romani], which may perhaps be regarded as evidence that the two bands had separated *before* these later Persian borrowings were absorbed into the speech of the western Gypsies' (emphasis added), but this modified position seems to have gone unnoticed, certainly by our late colleague Angus Fraser (1992: 39), who wrote:

> [D]espite Sampson's insistence that both sprang from a single source, some of Domari's dissimilarities from European Romani create doubts about how far we can assume that the parent community was uniform.

Sampson's position had moved to his *not* actually insisting that Romani and Domari sprang from a single source, and his basis for this radical shift – the Persian component of both – led me to examine it in an article that appeared in 1995. If there had been one migration that had remained intact through Persian territory before dividing, we would expect the Persian words acquired to be shared by all three languages, but there are surprisingly few: just 16 per cent between Romani and Domari, 7 per cent between Romani and Lomavren, and 12 per cent between Lomavren and Domari. And there are virtually none at all shared by all three. There are other lexical differences; most Iranic items in Domari are Kurdish, not Persian, while Lomavren has just one possibly Kurdish item. Romani has about ten. There is no Armenian or Greek in Domari, nor is there a trace of Greek in Lomavren, although that language is the second largest contributor to pre-European Romani after the Indic. And while only about one sixth of the Iranic-derived items in Romani are shared by Domari, over a half of them are found in Urdu.

Published estimates of the dates of the exodus differ remarkably, from as early as the fifth to as late as the fourteenth century. Also a matter of contention is the question of whether it consisted of one ready-formed group that left all at once, or several unrelated smaller groups that left over a long period of time. It is possible to determine the earliest date, however, by examining the language, which has features that clearly put its origin at no earlier than about the year 1000 CE. It was then that the neuter gender was becoming lost. Indic languages began with three (masculine, feminine and neuter) but, like the Romance languages developing out of Latin, they lost the neuter category, which got redistributed to the other two genders. Romani has only two genders, and did not leave India at an earlier time with three. Domari on the other hand does have three.

This fact provides us with the bottom end of a window in time; the upper end is when Romanies first appeared in the West, which was during the twelfth or thirteenth century. Thus we have a span of about two centuries during which to account for the move out of India, across the Middle East and up into Europe.

The high proportion of Persian items shared between Romani and Urdu, which contrasts with those shared among Romani, Domari and Lomavren, together with what we know about the origins of that language, suggested to me that a specific connection linked the two of them. Urdu began as a military lingua franca in the early medieval camps – in fact the word 'Urdu' itself *means* 'military camp' – and an examination of the semantic areas in the Romani vocabulary reveals a surprising number of military, or military-related, words of Indic origin, considering the proportionately small Indic-derived lexicon overall.

Taking into account other clues in the language, such as the words for non-Romanies which mean such things as 'prisoner', 'slave' and so on, and the oral traditions referring to a history involving warfare, it seemed logical to examine Indian history for further clues in this area. There were of course already several hypotheses in the literature. A military origin for Romanies, generally as captives, is not a new idea; De Goeje (1876: 32) wrote that:

> In the year 1000, we find bands of Zotts in the army of Abû-Naçr ibn-Bakhtiyâr, in Persia and Kirmân (Ibno-'l-Athîr, ix., p. 114). In 1025, al-Mançûra was conquered by Mahmûd al-Gaznawî, because the prince of this town had forsaken Islamism.

Clarke (1878: 134) wrote that:

> It was from the Ghaznevide conqueror and at home that the independence of the Jats received its death-blow. The victorious army

of Mahmoud, when returning laden with spoil from the Somnauth expedition of 1025, was attacked and pillaged by them on the banks of the Indus. Their temerity was chastised with exemplary rigour. Broken and dispersed by the resistless arms of the Sultan of Ghazni, they were not, however, annihilated.

arrow	*sulica*	< Skt śūla, Hi sūl
axe	*tover*	< Hi tarvar sword, Kurdish *taver*
battle	*kurripen*	< Skt ku- + -tvana
confront	*nikl-*	< Skt nikālayati, Hi nikālnā
encounter, engage-	*lat(h)*	< Skt labdha-, Hi laddhiya-
conqueror	*idjavno*	< Skt -nayati + karoti-
decamp	*rad-*	< Skt rah- + dadā
defeat in battle	*vidjav-*	*cf.* Hi vijit, vijetā
ditch	*xar, xavoj*	< Skt khata-, Hi khawa
fight	*kurr-*	< Skt kuayati, Hi kuna
gaiters	*patava*	< Skt patta-, Hi pa, *cf.* E. *puttees*
horse	*khuro*	< Skt ghoa-, Hi ghoā
military	*lurdikano*	< Skt lūati + -(k)ano
plunder	*lur-*	< Skt lūati, Hi lūnā, . E. *loot, Luri*
set up camp	*lod-*	< Skt lagyati
shot	*karja*	< Skt karika-
slaughter	*manušvari*	< Skt mānuamārikā
soldier	*kuripaskero*	< Skt kuayati + -tvana + kro
soldier	*lur, lurdo*	< Skt lūati, Hi lūnā
spear, lance	*bust*	< Skt vścika-, bhrśti- (now 'spit')
spear, stab	*pošav-*	< Skt sparśayā, Hi phasnā
sword	*xanrro*	< Skt khaaka-, Hi khā:ā
trident	*trušul*	< Skt triśūla- (now 'cross')
whip	*čukni, čupni*	< Skt čuknuti
	Of Iranic origin	
battleaxe	*nidjako*	< Persian naĵak, *cf.* also Kurdish nijakh
halter	*ašvar*	< Persian abzūr
saddle	*zen*	< zēn
spur	*buzex*	< Persian sbux
Indic Items in Romani with a military or a likely military association		

13

Leland, (1882: 24) wrote that 'Jat warriors were supplemented by other tribes ... they were broken and dispersed in the eleventh century by Mahmoud' and Burton (1898: 212) wrote that 'Sultan Mahmoud carried with him in AD 1011 some two hundred thousand [Indian] captives, the spoils of his expedition.' Kochanowski (1968: 27–8) later agreed that 'our own inter-disciplinary studies have shown that the Gypsies are Rajputs who left northern India,' and Vijender Bhalla's serological studies undertaken in India concluded that 'Rajputs occupy the [genetic] position nearest the Gypsies' (1992: 331–2). Nagy et al. conclude that there were 'non-significant differences' in haplotype frequencies between Haryana and Sikh Jats and Slovakian Roma, but 'significant differences with non-Romani populations' (2007: 19). Seventeen years ago the Polish scholar Lech Mróz had also considered a specific connection with the Islamic raids into India, saying 'I consider it likely that the Gypsies' ancestors arrived in Iran in the time of Mahmud of Ghazni, as a result of his raids into India' (1992: 40), and Bajram Haliti (2006: 6) has come to the same conclusion:

> Some time between the tenth and eleventh centuries, the largest groups of Roma left India and the main cause was invasion of the great emperor Mahmud Gazni, who led 17 raids in western India. Running away from terror, Roma first stopped in Iran, and then separated in two groups, the first moving toward Spain, and the second toward Byzantium and Greece.

It is significant, I think, that the Banjara, an Indian population some of whom claim descent from the Rajputs, include in their own historical record a number of references to their ancestors having been defeated by the Ghaznavids and taken out of India never to return. They believe that those were the ancestors of the Romanies.

Nevertheless there continues to be resistance to this; in 2004 in his own interpretation of Romani history, Viorel Achim wrote, '[t]he distinguishing feature of the Gypsy migration is that it was not of a military nature' and Tcherenkov and Laederich (*Ibid.*: 13) wrote that 'some authors claim that Rroma originated from either one of the upper castes such as the Rajputs or from a mix of different castes. With our current knowledge, this cannot be settled to satisfaction'. For some historians a more casual explanation is preferred; Solsten and McClure (1994: 6) write that '[p]referring to feel free and unhindered, Gypsies attached little importance to the accumulation of property and wealth, choosing instead a life of wandering'.

I personally am entirely convinced that we are on the right track with this emerging history. I see our ancestors as consisting of (a) an Indian military body accompanied by its camp followers that left India either in pursuit of invading Ghaznavids or as their captives, and (b) Indian slave-soldiers or *ghulams*, and perhaps mercenaries, being used on the side of the Ghaznavids. I believe that the Indian prisoners of war and another captive population – the Seljuqs, with whom the Ghaznavids were also engaged – were able to join forces and defeat their captors in AD 1038. The Seljuqs then brought the Indians with them as allies to defeat the Kingdom of Armenia, which they did in AD 1071. They established the Sultanate of Rûm in Anatolia, where the Indians were able to establish semi-autonomous areas known as *beyliks*, thus ensuring their continued cohesiveness as a group. For the next two centuries the Romani people and the Romani language began to take shape.

I want to comment here on the perhaps deliberate focusing of some writers on my reference to the Rajputs. Fonseca, for example, interprets my position as though I believe that our ancestors consisted solely of Rajputs. In her influential book *Bury Me Standing* she says:

> Gypsy writers and activists … argue for a classier genealogy; we hear, for example, that the Gypsies descend from the Kshattriyas, the warrior caste, just below the Brahmins. There is something ambiguous about origins, after all; you can be whoever you want to be (1996: 100).

Let me make it clear once again that in the make-up of medieval armies in that part of the world, the camp followers greatly outnumbered the actual militia, and the camp followers moreover included women as well as men. Our ancestors were not Rajputs. There was a minority of Rajputs among them.

Some, such as Leland, have tried to place our language somewhere among the seven Indian dialect groups, but have concluded that Proto-Romani belonged to another, now vanished, category of its own, because it matches no single one of them. Rather than supposing the existence of a vanished Prakrit from which Romani descends, however, the evidence points to a *mixed* origin, emerging from a *mixed* population in a *mixed* military environment. The military factor, evident from the social and historical clues, is also supported in the vocabulary, discussed earlier. The componental nature of the language also parallels the military origins of Urdu, the contact language that emerged as the lingua franca of the camps from a number of Indian and Dardic languages and from Persian, which was the language of administration not only in the Indian armies but also in the Ghaznavid and Seljuq armies as well. Clough (1876: 15) says that the military leaders:

experienced some difficulty in communicating with their new subjects. A lingua franca was composed, consisting principally of corrupt Persian and Hindi, and this was known under the name of *Urdu Zeban*, or camp language, to distinguish it from the court language, but the poets called it *Rekhta*, or 'scattered,' on account of the variety of elements composing it.

Romani clearly demonstrates its mixed Indian origin with the considerable number of synonyms it contains. It has three Indian words for 'sing', for example, and three for 'scare' and 'burn', two for 'wash' and 'cold', and so on – none shared by any single language spoken in India. There are even three, or possibly four, different dialect groups represented in the numerals alone; Vijay John in Texas is doing valuable research in this area. Thus the contact language that formed the basis of Romani, and which for lack of a name I have called *Rajputic* was, like its speakers themselves, drawn from a number of ethno-linguistic populations, and maintained that composite identity until reaching Anatolia. This too has attracted criticism, predictably from Matras, who in a recent book (Margalit and Matras 2008: 107) writes:

> Despite Hancock's claims about the existence of linguistic findings to support this – although he has never produced them – there is no evidence, and certainly no linguistic proof, to support the theory of … a Romani melting pot outside of India.

Matras' position must therefore be understood as stating that Romani was ready-formed inside India, and was taken out of India by *one* people speaking that *one* language – his 'itinerant castes of artisans and entertainers' and 'who appear to have been members of service-providing castes, similar in status and occupational profile to jatis or service groups known in some parts of India as dom' – although he doesn't explain how those groups presumably reassembled and how and why they reached Anatolia in the tenth century.

To return to the question of identity, I have argued elsewhere that, like our language, this came into being during the sedentary Anatolian period. The professional status of the Indians contributed to the contact variety of their language, which crystallised into the Romani language and its people, who were particularly under the influence of Byzantine Greek. While a case may be made for the word *R(r)om* being derived from *dom* its semantics have been challenged by Kenrick (1994: 37), who maintains that it meant simply 'man', or 'our people' rather than 'others', and, at the time of the exodus from India, did not have Brockhaus and Sinclair's later interpretation. Leitner (1877: *i*–6) has also shown that, in some Dardic languages, the words *rōm* and *rŏm* mean simply 'race of people', in Khowar it means a 'flock' (Sloan 1981: 128), while Mookerji (1927: 66) says that in Bihari, 'the epithet for a *gentleman* is *Rouma*, a contraction of the Sanskrit *Romya* (the beautiful)'. Some of the Indians probably were *dom* in India, and while we might make a case for convergence, it is in my opinion more likely that the self-designation *R(r)om* originated in the names applied generally to citizens of the Byzantine Empire: *Romaivi, Romitoi*. There *were* no 'Rom' before Anatolia.

I should like to advance here a different perspective which, I believe, provides an alternative way of understanding the question of identity, as well as why the question of identity confuses journalists and sociologists, and why it causes us ourselves so much of a problem.

In light of the particular details of our origins and of our shared and unshared social history since then, certain conclusions must be drawn: first, that the population has been a composite one from its very beginning, and at that time was occupationally rather than ethnically defined; second, that while the earliest components – linguistic, cultural and genetic – are traceable to India, we essentially constitute a population that acquired our identity and language in the West (accepting the Christian, Greek-speaking Byzantine Empire as being linguistically and culturally 'western'), and, third, that the entry into Europe from what is today Turkey was not as a single people, but as a number of smaller migrations over perhaps as much as a two-century span of time. These factors have combined to create a situation that is in some sense unique, that is to say, we are a population of Asian origin that has spent essentially the entire period of our existence in the West, and which, because of our mixed origins, has been open to absorbing and assimilating various non-Romani western peoples, contradictory perhaps in light of the stringent cultural restrictions on socialising with non-Romanies – an anomaly that bears examination.

Because the population was fragmenting and moving into Europe during the very period that an ethnic identity was emerging, there is no sense of our ever having been a single, unified people in one place at one time. We can speak of a 'core of direct retention' consisting of genetic, linguistic and cultural factors traceable to Asia and evident to a greater or lesser extent in all populations identifying as Romani, but we must also acknowledge that all of these factors have been augmented through contact with European peoples and cultures, and it is the latter accretions that account for the sometimes extreme differences from group to group. The Romanies in Spain have been separated from those in Romania for perhaps six centuries, and by 2,000 kilometres in distance. In Europe the migration, by this time consisting of a conglomerate ethnic population moving off in different directions at different times and whose diverse speech had become one language in a multiplicity of dialects, encountered other mobile populations and in some cases joined and intermarried with them. Sometimes the Romani cultural and linguistic presence was sufficiently overwhelming that the newly encountered populations were absorbed and became Romanies in subsequent generations; sometimes the Romani contribution was not sufficient to maintain itself, and other non-Romani populations such as the Jenisch or the Quinquis emerged. This last factor underlies some of the discussion here today.

For some groups, 'core' Romani culture has been diluted practically out of existence, sometimes by deliberate government policy as in eighteenth-century Hungary or Spain, yet such populations are nevertheless regarded as 'Gypsies' by the larger society on the basis of appearance, dress, name, occupation and neighbourhood and are treated accordingly. They have, however, no traditional ethnic community in which to find refuge. Like urbanised, detribalised Native Americans, or like Chicanos who do not speak Spanish and who regard themselves as neither Mexican nor Anglo-American, in some respects they have become 'new' ethnic groups: unable to speak the ancestral language and unfamiliar with traditional culture and behaviour, yet still distinct from the larger population and shunned by it. At the other extreme are Romani populations in substantial numbers, such as the Vlax or Sinti, who vigorously maintain the language and the culture and who are restrained from functioning in the European mainstream because of them.

As we acquire our own voice I see a rising wall of resistance to it from the outside; our effort to become educated and to speak for ourselves is clearly perceived as a threat to those who support globalism and the assimilation of disruptive ethnic populations. Non-Romani organisations have been created to study and define Romani populations, even to cultivate our thinkers and our leaders. The Open Society Institute has a scholarship programme 'to support the creation of a broad-based Roma elite'.

Non-Romanies exercising an intellectual authority over our people decide on the standardisation of our language, and non-Romanies have represented them-selves as our political spokesmen. Non-Romanies in their droves have decided that arranged early-teen marriage among Vlax Romanies is reprehensible, although no similar outrage has been directed at India where it is also common and where the Romani custom originated. Likewise arranged marriages amongst the European royal families have taken place for centuries without moral criticism, although ours are periodically an issue in the western press.

Remarkably, the Council of Europe has released an 'official' account of our history (Wogg, 2006), something they would scarcely do any for any other nation:

what would the Germans or Russians say if an official history and description had been imposed upon them without their having been once consulted? My last quote from Yaron Matras was from a book that has recently appeared called *The Roma: A Minority in Europe*, edited by Roni Stauber and Raphael Vago and published by the Central European University Press. It contains the papers from the first international conference on the Roma at Tel Aviv University in Israel held in December 2002. No Romanies participated in either the presentations or the organisation of that conference. This is to me a colossal insult and a mark of supreme arrogance. It is also an indication of the direction things are surely taking if we do not protest now, and loudly. That such conferences on Romani issues can be organised without any Romani involvement whatsoever is reminiscent of meetings of the US Bureau of Indian Affairs in the early 1900s where Native American issues were discussed in the absence of any Indian participation or representation; a Black Studies conference with no African American presence would be unthinkable; a Jewish policy symposium with no Jewish voice would be an outrage. Academics and politicians who have never met a Romani in their lives make their opinions about Romani policy known in the national press. At the same time some of the same people who *have* met us seem to feel threatened by those of us who are educated or who are branded as 'activists', as though this were automatically a bad thing, thereby wasting the resource potential of such marginalised individuals when so few Romanies educated to degree level exist. When I first met David Crowe, a US Holocaust Memorial Council consultant on the Romani Holocaust, his very first words were: 'I'm not going to be intimidated by you'. At the University of Texas in April 2007, the promotional flyer for a conference on Romani women in Turkey entitled *Reconfiguring gender and Roma ('Gypsy') identity through political discourses in Western Turkey* noted that 'Rom and non-Rom men's voices speak for Roma women', although the 'reconfiguration of Roma identity' in this presentation was made on our behalf by a *non*-Romani woman, and not by a Romani herself. We recently acquired an addition to the Romani Archives, presently at the University of Texas, a report by an associate professor of anthropology at DePaul University in Chicago, who went to Croatia 'for the purpose of establishing a Romani woman's empowerment program' (Hofman, 2008: 46). By her own admission she knew nothing about Romanies, and she wasn't successful – at least not in helping us. But she did get a travel grant and a publication out of it.

A week-long 'Gypsy' conference at the University of Florida in March 2007 consisted mainly of singing, dancing and dressing up by various non-Roma, but included no Romani participation. When they were questioned in this regard, the response was that they 'couldn't find any Gypsies'. They have since received a complaint from members of the Miami Romani community. When the late Miles Lerman called me at home in 1998 before I took up my position on the US Holocaust Memorial Council he nervously asked, 'Are you an activist?' This scary word 'activist' comes from 'act', and we must act now. I was so pleased that the Romany and Traveller Family History Society was established and is growing, the first organisation of its kind created by and for Romanies. Initiatives such as this bring the beginning of change. Surely if groups or individuals who identify themselves as Romanies seek to assert their ethnicity, and to ally themselves with others similarly motivated, then this is entirely their own business. The non-Romani anthropologists, sociologists, folklorists and others who have taken upon themselves the role of ethnic police are interfering and presumptuous at best, and are perpetuating paternalistic attitudes. Something more sinister underlies the marginalisation of our educated Romanies who argue for ethnic unification: it flies directly in the face of those who seek to control and regiment the world's peoples and economies. I call for a new respect and a new cooperation between Romanies and *gadje*, and an end to the nineteenth-century cultural colonialism and neo-Gypsylorism that lives on in only slightly modified guise.

Before closing I do want to take this opportunity to speak out – yet again – against our national sickness, commented on over 130 years ago by George Smith of Coalville who said 'almost all Gipsies have an inveterate hatred and jealousy towards each other, especially if one sets himself up as knowing more than [another] in the next yard' (1880: 195). Salunke (1989: 28) saw it as being a characteristic of our distant military ancestors, whose 'major vice [is] the main reason which does not allow them to come together and try to solve their problems. For minor disputes they never try to come together and negotiate to thrash out their problems or to resolve some reforms; the superiority of their kinsmen seems to be intolerable to them'. Thus it is very deeply rooted in our history. We all recognise this and we all deplore it; yet if we are to regain control of our own affairs we must put this aside and learn to cooperate with each other. Our detractors delight in watching our infighting, and see it as evidence that we are not ready to play with the big boys.

Summary

1   The linguistic features of Romani identify it as a new-Indic language rather than an old-Indic language, dating its time of separation from India at no earlier than ca. AD 1000.

2   The Romani language cannot be traced to any single Prakritic branch of the Indic languages but has features from several of them, although it is

most like those of the Central group. The language closest to Romani is Urdu which itself emerged from Rajputic.

3   Romani includes a substantial Dardic component (particularly from Phalura) and items from Burushaski, a language isolate spoken in the Pamir and nowhere else. This, and other linguistic evidence, points to an exodus through this particular area – the same area through which the Ghaznavids moved into and out of India.

4   The various Romani terms for non-Romani peoples suggest a military/non-military relationship; thus *gadžo* is traceable to an original Sanskrit form (*gajjha*) which means 'civilian', *das* and *goro* both mean 'slave, enemy, captive', and *gomi* means 'one who has surrendered'.

5   Romani has a military vocabulary of Indian origin, including the words for 'soldier', 'sword', 'attack', 'spear', 'trident', 'battle cry' and 'gaiters'. On the other hand, most of its non-military vocabulary relating to metalworking or agriculture, for example, consists of words not originating in India.

6   Some Romani groups in Europe today maintain the emblems of the Sun and the Moon as well as the *nadjakor* mattock as identifying insignia, all of which had the same function for the Rajputs.

7   Cultural practices of some Romani groups in Europe today resemble elements of Shaktism or goddess worship, as in the Rajputs' worship of the warrior goddess Parvati, another name for Kali/Durga. The European pre-eminence of *Les Saintes-Maries* may be taken to indicate a certain cultural affinity (Fraser, *Ibid.*: 313). The statue of Kali may be said to be immersed in the Mediterranean just as it is in the Ganges once a year in India. The Hindu deities Vayu and Maruti are mentioned in some Romani proverbs.

8   Throughout the earliest fifteenth- and sixteenth-century written records we find that Romanies told the Europeans that they had been defeated after conflicts with Islamic forces (Fraser, *Ibid.*: 72, 83). We should recall that the period after the Muslim invasion of India was also a period in which Byzantines, Crusaders and Armenians sustained a patchwork of anti-Islamic military resistance in Anatolia, with the last Armenian principality being reduced by the Ottomans as late as 1361. The oral tradition of some Romani groups in Europe includes stories of a conflict with Islam leading to the original migration west.

9   The mixed linguistic nature of Romani is evident from the numbers of synonyms of Indic origin in modern Romani, for example, the multiple words for 'wash', 'burn', 'awaken', 'back', 'dog', 'fight', 'belt', 'give', 'birth',

'arise', 'bracelet', 'cold', 'comb', 'day', 'excreta', 'fear', 'food', 'heel', 'leave', 'man', 'move', 'non-Romani', 'open', 'pay', 'sing', 'straw', 'thin', 'tomorrow' 'raw', 'wet' and so on.

10 Our population has been a composite one from its very beginning and at the beginning was occupationally, rather than ethnically, defined.

11 While our earliest linguistic, cultural and genetic components are traceable to India, Romanies everywhere essentially constitute a population that acquired its identity and language in the West (accepting the Christian, Greek-speaking Byzantine Empire as linguistically and culturally Western).

12 The entry into Europe from Anatolia was not as a single people, but as a number of smaller migrations, at the least three, over perhaps as much as a two-century span of time.

References

ab Hortis, Samuel Augustini. 1775–6. 'Von den heutigen Zustande, sonderbaren Sitten und Lebensart, wie auch von den übriben Eigenschaften und Umständen der Zigeuner in Ungarn,' *Zeitschrift Kaiserlich Königliche Allergnädigste Privilegierte Anzeigen aus Sämtlichen Kaiserlich Königliche. Erbländer*, 1:159–416, 2:7-159.

Achim, Viorel. 2004. *The Roma in Romanian History*. Budapest: Central European University Press.

Bhalla, Vijender. 1992. 'Ethnicity and Indian origins of Gypsies of Eastern Europe and the USSR: a bio-Anthropological-perspective', in K. Singh, ed., *Ethnicity, Caste and People*, private, Moscow & Delhi.

Burton, Sir Richard. 1898. *The Jew, the Gypsy and El Islam*. Hollywood: The Angriff Press.

Clarke, A. 1878. 'Origin and wanderings of the Gypsies'. *The Edinburgh Review*, 148:117–146.

Colocci, Adrian. 1907. Review of De Goeje (1903). *Journal of the Gypsy Lore Society*, new series, 1:278–80.

Clough, James Cresswell. 1876. *On the Existence of Mixed Languages*. London: Longmans. Green and Co.

De Goeje, Michiel J. 1875. *Mémoire sur les Migrations des Tsiganes travers l'Asie*. Mémoires d'Histoire et de Géographie Orientales, No. 3, Leiden: Brill.

Finck, Franz N. 1907. *Die Sprache der armenischen Zigeuner*. St. Petersburg: Imperial Science Academy.

Fonseca, Isabel. 1996. *Bury Me Standing: The Gypsies and their Journey*. New York: Random House.

Fraser, Angus. 1992. *The Gypsies*. Oxford: Blackwell.

Grellmann, Heinrich. 1783. *Historischer Versuch über die Zigeuner*. Göttingen: Dietrich Verlag. English translation, 1807.

Haliti, Bajram. 2006. *India and Roma*. Kosovo: Central Office of Roma.

Hancock, Ian. 1992. 'The Hungarian student Vályi István and the Indian connection of Romani'. *Roma*, 36:46–9.

Heimlich, Evan. 1994. 'Gypsy Americans' in J. Galens, A. Sheets and R. Young, eds., *Gale Encyclopedia of Multicultural America*. New York: Gale Research, Inc. pp. 627–40.

Higgie, Brenda. 1984. *Proto-Romanes Phonology*. Unpublished doctoral dissertation. Austin: University of Texas.

Hoade, Eugene. 1952. *Western Pilgrims*. Studium Biblicum Franciscanum, Paper No. 18, Jerusalem.

Hofman, Nila Ginger. 2008. 'Accessing Romani women study participants: collaborating with their gatekeepers and other NGO entrepreneurs'. *Practicing Anthropology*, 30(3):46–9.

Horvath, Julia, and Paul Wexler, eds., 1998. *Relexification in Creole and non-Creole Languages, with Special Attention to Haitian Creole, Modern Hebrew, Romani and Rumanian*. Wiesbaden: Harrassowitz.

John, Vijay. 2006. *Indian Origins of Romani Numbers: A Case for KoVnJization*. Romani Studies term paper, University of Texas, Fall semester.

Kaufman, Terrence. 1984. *Explorations in Proto-Gypsy Phonology and Classification*. Paper presented at the Sixth South Asian Languages Analysis Round table. Austin.

Kenrick, Donald. 1994. *Les Tsiganes, de l'Inde à la Méditerranée*. Paris: Centre de Recherches Tsiganes.

Kenrick, Donald. 2000. 'Learning Domari: Unit 2.' *Kuri-DR Journal*, 1(3):2–5.

Kochanowski, Vania de Gila. 1968. 'Black Gypsies, white Gypsies,' *Diogenes*, 63:2–47.

Leitner, G.W. 1877. *The Languages and Races of Dardistan*. Lahore: The Government Printing Office.

Leland, Charles Godfrey. 1882. *The Gypsies*. New York: Houghton, Mifflin and Co.

Liégeois, Jean-Pierre. 1986. *Gypsies: an Illustrated History*. London: Al-Saqi Books.

Margalit, G. and Y. Matras. 2008. 'Gypsies in Germany – German Gypsies? Identity and politics of Sinti and Roma in Germany', in R. Stauber and R. Vago, eds. 2008. *The Roma: A Minority in Europe*. Budapest: Central European University Press. pp. 103–16.

Matras, Yaron, ed. 1995. *Romani in Contact: The History, Structure and Sociology of a Language*. Amsterdam: John Benjamins.

Matras, Yaron. 1999. 'The state of present-day Domari in Jerusalem,' *Mediterranean Language Review*, 11:1–58.

Matras Y. 2004. 'Typology, dialectology and the structure of complementation in Romani' in B. Kortmann, ed. *Dialectology meets typology*. Berlin: Mouton. pp. 277–304.

Mookerji, Bhudeb. 1927. 'The Gipsies and the spread of Indian culture,' *Journal of the Department of Letters*, 15:61–4. Calcutta: University of Calcutta.

Mróz, Lech. 1992. *Geneza Cyganów i Ich Kultury.* Warsaw: Wydawnictwa Fundacji 'Historia Pro Futuro'.

Münster, Sebastian. 1544. *Cosmographiae Universalis*. Paris.

Muratori, Ludovico A. 1752–4. *Annali d'Italia*. Rome: Barbiellini.

Nagy, M., Henke, L., Henke, J., Chatthopadhyay, P., *et al.,* 2007. 'Searching for the origin of Romanies: Slovakian Romani, Jats of Haryana and Jat Sikhs Y-STR data in comparison with different Romani populations'. *Forensic Science International,* 169(1): 19–26.

Paspati, A. 1883. *Etudes sur les Tchingianés ou Bohémiens de l'Empire Ottoman.* Constantinople: Koromélia.

Piasere, Leonardo. 1988. 'De origine cinganorum,' in P. H. Stahl, ed. *Recueil: Etudes et Documents Balkaniques et Méditerranéens*. pp. 105–26.

Pott, Augustus F. 1844–5. *Die Zigeuner in Europa und Asien*. Two volumes. Halle: Heynemann Verlag.

Rüdiger, Johann. 1782. *Neuester Zuwachs der Teuschen, Fremden und Allgemeinen Sprachkunde in Einigen Aufsatzen, Bücheranzeigen und Nachrichten.* Vol. 1. Leipzig.

Salunke, N. B. 1989. 'The Rajput Lohars'. *Roma*, 30: 21–31.

Sampson, John. 1923. 'On the origin and early migration of the Gypsies'. *Journal of the Gypsy Lore Society*, third series, 2(4):156–169.

Sampson, John. 1926. *The Dialect of the Gypsies of Wales*. Oxford: Clarendon Press.

Sinclair, Albert T. 1909. 'The word "Rom"'. *Journal of the Gypsy Lore Society*, New Series, 3:33–42.

Sirimarco, Elizabeth. 2000. *Endangered Cultures: Gypsies*. Mankato: Smart Apple Media.

Sloan, Samuel. 1981. *Khowar-English Dictionary: A Dictionary of the Predominant Language of Chitral*. Peshawar: Frontier Printing Corporation.

Smith, George. 1880. *Gipsy Life*. London: Haughton.

Solsten, Eric and McClure, David. 1994. *Austria: a Country Study*. Washington: Library of Congress Federal Research Division.

Starkie, Walter. 1972. 'Gypsies: The eternal travellers,' introduction to Leon Petulengro. *Romany Recipes and Remedies*. Hollywood: Newcastle Publishing Co. pp. *i–iv*.

Sway, Marlene. 1988. *Familiar Strangers: Gypsy Life in America*. Urbana: University of Illinois Press.

Tálos, Endre. 1999. 'Etymologica Zingarica'. *Acta Linguistica Hungarica*, 46:215–268.

Tcherenkov, Lev and Laederich, Stéphane. 2004. *The Rroma*. Basel. Schwabe. Two volumes.

Turner, Ralph L. 1927. 'On the position of Romani in Indo-Aryan', *Journal of the Gypsy Lore Society*. 3rd Series, 5(4):145–83.

Turner, Ralph L. 1966. *A Comparative Dictionary of the Indo-Aryan Languages*. London: Oxford Univ. Press.

Wogg, Michael, (ed). 2006. *Roma History: From India to Europe*. Strasbourg. Council of Europe Directorate General IV, Education of Roma Children in Europe.

2

The Gypsies in Turkey: history, ethnicity and identity – an action research strategy in practice*

Dr Adrian Marsh

Södertorns University College,
Stockholm

Origins: the Romanlar, Domlar, and Lomlar

Do origins matter? Or are they just a narrativisation, a projection backwards of current ideologies of identity? Or can we turn this question on its head and ask what revisions of the historical narrative new awarenesses of identity and oppression require, and how the new ways of making sense of the historical record free community action from older ideological constraints? In the previous paper Hancock has shown how the 'Gypsy' groups of Turkey, (Romani, Domari, Lomavren and Travellers) have different linguistic histories and points of origin. But, as with people of African origin in North America, a common experience of racism or discrimination may forge commonalities of identity and action.

The first apparent reference to 'Gypsies' in Istanbul is from the eleventh century, when a group described as Atsinganoi, 'a Sarmatian people' and the descendants of Simon the Magician, came to the court of the Byzantine Basileus (emperor) Constantine IX Monomachus circa AD 1050 (Marsh, 2008). They were asked by the emperor to help him rid the royal hunting park, the Philopation (outside of the Blachernai Palace, Tekfür Sarayi, close to modern-day Sulukule in Istanbul) of wild beasts that were killing the deer and other game animals. The Atsinganoi obliged, but when they returned to the emperor to claim payment, the monk (later Saint) George the Athonite

---

* This paper goes beyond the discussion of origins given at the seminar, much of which is covered by Hancock in his paper, to discuss the implications of a new awareness of common interests and origins for community action.

of Iviron denounced them as sorcerers. Making the sign of the cross over a dog they had 'charmed', he challenged them as false prophets and teachers of 'devilish things'.

We cannot be sure whether these Atsiganoi were Domari or Romani. The Dom may have arrived earlier, having founded a short-lived state in the Mesopotamian region in the ninth century that was eventually defeated by the Abbasids and Byzantines: they almost certainly appear in Antioch (Antakya) circa AD 1040 in a confrontation with the Antiochenes and their caravan. The earliest mention of the Lom has not been definitively discussed by scholars yet.

The presence of 'Gypsies' if we use that word to translate the terms *Atsinganoi* (a kind of Christian heretic) and *Aiguptoi* (Egyptians) by the Byzantines, is well documented from the twelfth to fifteenth centuries, as they worked as soothsayers, fortune-tellers, snake charmers, acrobats and entertainers in Constantinople. They called themselves Romitoi or 'Roman' (the equivalent of the modern Turkish 'Romanlar'). They were also present as shoemakers, basket makers, knife makers and metalworkers in the lands of Greece, Bulgaria, Macedonia, Kosovo, Serbia and Bosnia. On the Ionian Islands of Lefkada and Zakynthos they were organised into war bands under license from the Venetian Republic and granted a measure of autonomy and tax privileges, although they do not seem to have been part of the Byzantine Emperor's armies.

They were present in the Ottoman forces (as the *Çingene sancak*) that took Constantinople in 1453 and were an important part of Ottoman society, known as Çingene or Kipti. They worked as basket makers, horse traders, metalworkers, tailors, shoemakers, puppeteers, dancers, musicians and entertainers, often organised in guilds with wealthy. Gypsies were even appointed to important offices on occasion. In the eighteenth century European 'orientalist' ideas and opinions began to influence the views of Ottoman officials negatively both about their Asian subjects and Gypsies (Marsh, 2008).

The Romanlar are a group to whom the European Roma (or Rroma) are directly related, sharing much in culture, language and economic specialisms. There are many subdivisions amongst the Romanlar, mostly defined by occupation (*sepetçiler*: basket makers; *kalayci*: tin smiths; *bokci*: pedlars; *hammanci*: bath attendants; *hamalci*: porters and carriers; *arabaci*: horse-drawn carriage and wagon drivers, and so on). The class system amongst the Romanlar means that the musicians (unlike in other countries such as Sweden or the UK) are frequently the élite. Most are Sunni Muslim in faith, but there are significant numbers of nomadic and settled Alevi (Shi'ite) Romanlar, particularly in the eastern part of the country and around the outskirts of Istanbul. They mostly occupy distinct *mahalles* or neighbourhoods, and are socially and economically discriminated against, and spatially segregated from wider Turkish society. They are organised with some 28 local associations and a national federation of Romanlar organisations. There are according to current research about four million Romanlar living in Turkey, many of whom speak one of four or five dialects of Romanes (Acton and Marsh, 2007).

The Domlar are related to groups of Dom Gypsies in the Middle East and may have arrived in the Turkish lands sometime in the early eleventh century AD in the south-east (Diyarbakir, Antakya, Mardin), if references in Armenian chronicles are correct. They currently live in southern and eastern parts of Turkey and are primarily musicians who specialise in playing the large drum (*davul*) and a kind of simple oboe (*zurna*). They maintain their own language Domari (or Domca in Turkish) and also speak Kurmanci or Zaza and Turkish, keeping Domari as a 'secret language' or in-group code. Culturally close to the Kurdish population, they nevertheless suffer significant and violent discrimination from them with documented cases of physical attacks and murder. They also suffer from the discriminatory attentions of the Turkish state security forces in the region. Most Dom are close to Sufi Islam and local sheikhs, but some are Yezidi in the north-east region close to Doğubayezit. There are some 500,000 in Turkey, although this figure needs further research to confirm. They are frequently extremely poor and many are nomadic.

The Lomlar's origins are extremely obscure and it may be that they represent a breakaway group that split from the Rom during the eleventh century. Not moving westwards, they remained in the east of Anatolia during the Saldjūk and Ottoman periods. The current Lom population is largely descended from those that were forced to move to Turkey in the ethnic cleansing carried out by the Russians in their conquest of the Caucasus in the 1870s. They now reside in small communities in the north-east and Black Sea region where they are referred to by the derogatory term 'Posha' (from *bo'* meaning 'empty' or 'stupid'). They are mostly settled and agricultural, although there are numbers who are professionals (although these, like all such Gypsies in Turkey, 'hide' their ethnicity). Some of them maintain their language, Lomavren, and a tradition of musicianship but many have 'lost' this and few under the age of 60 speak the language fluently. There are possibly 150,000 of them but numbers are very hard to estimate.

The Geygelli, Gezginler and other Göcebe groups

There are a number of 'Travellers' amongst the Gypsy communities of Turkey that are primarily nomadic for large parts of the year, often identified as 'Yörüks' in ethnographic studies. Most are Alevi; some that have settled have 'become'

Alevi and deny a Gypsy heritage (although they speak contact languages using elements of Romanes, such as the Alevis in Kuştepe in Istanbul or the Geygelli nomads of central Anatolia). There are also some groups that have adopted other identities, who originate in Gypsy communities from the medieval period but no longer identify with them. They are very much on the margins of Turkish society and no estimates of their numbers can be made. In Thrace they are known by a variety of names including Mangösür and Çalgar and other Gypsy communities do not, by and large, marry with or into these groups.

Starting the new action research

The 'Promoting Roma (Gypsy) Rights in Turkey' research project began in May 2006 with training workshops conducted by the Centre for Migration Research (CMR) at Istanbul Bilgi University. However, unforeseen difficulties prevented the CMR from continuing with the project, and the research plan, methodology and missions were reorganised and rescheduled by the coordinator to recommence in August 2006. The first phase of the research missions sent researchers to Izmir, Manisa, Balikesir, Bursa, Ankara, Kirikkale, Küçükbakkalköy, Kağithane and Kuştepe in Istanbul.

Research was also continued in the Sulukule neighbourhood of Istanbul, research that had started under a research programme funded by the Economic and Social Research Council (ESRC) and carried out by the University of Greenwich with the title 'Charting the variety of aspirations amongst Gypsy groups in Turkey' in June 2006 (ESRC Ref *RES-000-22-1652*). This successful partnership cooperating with other non-governmental organisations (NGOs) such as the Accessible Life Foundation, the Human Settlements Association and Platform Arts Centre meant that a network of action research developed, with a synergy between the academic knowledge-oriented goals of the university sponsors and the policy goals of the NGO sponsors.

The data from the first two phases of the CMR research project were important in terms of building a solid database of information about the economic, social and cultural situation of the Romanlar communities but lacked more concrete evidence to provide a basis for active advocacy specifically related to human rights abuses. There was also no research carried out amongst the other Gypsy groups in Turkey as yet.

The third phase of the CMR research project began in late October 2006 with a mission to the Diyarbakir area to locate the Dom Gypsies of the region and to collect data regarding issues facing them, in the context of the difficulties and conflicts that have been present in the region for many years. The mission was undertaken by the CMR project coordinators and researchers in partnership with Professor Thomas Acton from the University of Greenwich, Idaver Mememdov from the European Roma Rights Centre (ERRC), and Gunnar Grut from Trondheim University College in Norway and a former member of the United Nations (UN) peacekeeping missions to Afghanistan and Lebanon.

Articulating Dom, Rom and Lom civic identities

The mission proved very successful in its aims of establishing contact with a previously unrecognised group, of initiating a relationship that broadened into one of support and capacity building, and of documenting a number of serious cases of discrimination involving Dom Gypsies. The mission carried out research in Diyarbakir, Silwan, Kiziltepe, Mardin, Nusaybin, Bitlis and Van, interviewing many settled and nomadic Domlar and Romanlar amounting to some 80 persons in all.

The third phase also continued with more research in Erzerum, Aşkale, Erzincan, Bodrum and Istanbul's Küçükbakkalköy, Kağithane and Sulukule neighbourhoods. In Istanbul demolition had destroyed much of the first two communities and threatened the latter. A further mission was sent to Izmir to further document the relationships between the competing Romanlar associations there, after a direct appeal for intervention from the Izmir Romanlar Association when they visited the offices of the hCa (Helsinki Citizen's Assembly) in Istanbul, following the earlier visit by researchers.

A further visit to Diyarbakir in November/December 2006 brought more detailed testimony to light of abuses of Dom at the hands of the local security forces and enabled the research team actively to support the founding of the first Dom association in Turkey.

The research moved into a new phase in January 2007 with work to identify the extent of diversity of religious affiliation amongst the Romanlar, and research in Kuştepe with the Romanlar and Alevi communities. The preparation for more in-depth research concerning women's health issues was undertaken with guidance from Dr Mustafa Özünal at Taksim General Hospital and the ERRC, following which a survey was drawn up and carried out in February in Edirne in partnership with one of the local schools, Cumhuriyet Ilkoğretim Okulu, and its head teacher, Ms Nezahat Satici.

In April 2007 another visit to Diyarbakir sought to confirm previous testimony regarding a case of the murder of two boys from a Roman family in Silwan (that sadly proved impossible without 'witness protection') and to seek the support of the Diyarbakir City authority for the new Dom Association, a venture that proved to be successful.

There were a number of developments in May 2007 as the research project moved further south to Adana and Mersin. The team participated in the symposium organised by the project managers and met with both the local Mersin Romanlar Association and the President of the National Federation Erdinç Çekiç to discuss the research and the findings thus far, and discuss what new directions the research might take. The mission also visited the Romanlar community of Ceyhan and identified an issue over lands rights where advocacy and legal help were required.

A further visit to Izmir was undertaken to both participate in the symposium organised there and to undertake research in the outlying areas of Çaybaşi, Tire and Çipri where small associations had begun to work with the support of the Izmir Modern Roman Association.

With the extension of the research project, the team undertook missions to Keşan as well as a further mission to Mersin and Adana to investigate the economic strategies that had been developed by the local association in the face of significant discrimination employment. There was a mission to Diyarbakir to develop what had been learned in Mersin and Adana in the context of the economic problems amongst the Dom communities. Also investigated were the possibility of micro-credit programmes amongst the Dom women and instances of abuse arising from intercommunal marriages between the Dom and Kurdish communities. A short mission to Izmit/Kocaeli sought to document the then pending demolition of a neighbourhood by the local authority, and the relationship between the local Muslim associations and the Romanlar community.

The final phase of the research project established contact with the Lomlar of the north-east of Turkey to carry out research amongst them. The missions in late August and early September 2007 visited Ağri, Kars, Şavşat, Artvin, Yüsüfeli, Trabzon, Rize, Ardeşen and Akcaabat in the Black Sea region. These two missions were successful in finding Lomlar communities that provided a wealth of data regarding discrimination and prejudices shown towards them by the majority society and in establishing contact between the national Romani federation (ROMDEF) and members of the Lom communities in Şavşat and Akcaabat, as well as between young Lom and the Roma Memorial University Scholarship (RMUSP) that resulted in a scholarship being awarded to a young Lom woman.

Assaults by police and local-authority security officers in Avcilar near Istanbul prompted a short mission to Avcilar and Tahtakale in early September 2007 to document the extent of these actions against nomadic Gypsies encamped in the area, and to investigate the possibility of making a referral for casework. The groups were in the first instance Dom from south-eastern

Turkey, and in the second Alevi Romanlar: both had been subject to assaults and the destruction of their camps in the most arbitrary and brutal fashions. Information was immediately passed on to the legal advisor to the project and further investigation alerted the research team to the existence of a camp for detainees where many Gypsies were taken after arrest in these instances in the Topkapi district of Istanbul. Gypsy street traders and pedlars from Istanbul were also frequently incarcerated in this detention centre.

Tackling discrimination in work

In September one man in Çorlu told researchers of his experiences with a restaurant job that took place some two years previously. He became the chief waiter in a restaurant employing between 20 or 30 persons. The other employees went to see the boss to complain and asked him, 'So what is this, a "gypsy" is to lord it over us…?' Yuksel eventually quit his job because he could not work in this kind of environment.

Also in Çorlu one young woman had applied for a job in a store but they did not employ her after learning where she lived as they automatically understood from this that she was a Gypsy. In order for her son to get a job in a factory, they found it necessary to give a false address.

Zafer Bey, an important figure in the local Roma association (Kirklarelli, September 2006), had applied to the Turkish navy school and passed the written, oral and physical exams. He was subsequently rejected without any explanation. When he called the General Command in Ankara he was told that he did not 'meet the necessary conditions'. When he asked for more details he was told that he should stop asking questions in order to avoid trouble.

Zafer wanted to take up this case legally but his application to do so was rejected by five different courts: the local court, a higher court, the military court, Ankara's tenth administrative court, and finally the Council of State (Danıştay). After his failure with the Turkish legal system, Zafer decided he wanted to take the case to the European Court of Human Rights. He felt that the Roma identity was excluded 'even though we are not terrorists'. The discrimination is of a general character, and also prevents them from getting jobs.

Problems in education and the health service

Before they were evicted in the infamous slum clearances, the Gypsy children of Sulukule in Istanbul were frequently forced to sit in separate rows in the classroom, according to the members of the Sulukule Romani Association that researchers spoke to in July 2006. This pattern was also one that researchers found in many areas of Turkey; researchers were told in Kağithane in Istanbul that children attend schools with non-Romani children in mixed classes, but Gypsy children are usually placed separately in the classrooms. The parents complained about this situation both to the teachers and the principal, but had received no response by September 2006.

In Küçükbakkalköy, Istanbul (October 2006), researchers spoke to an eight-year-old girl of her experience of school. She told them she was always seated in the last row, furthest away from the teacher. The little girl admitted she sometimes had hearing difficulties and that it was hard to concentrate when sitting at the back of the classroom. The little girl also told researchers that once she had actually dared to ask the teacher if she could sit in the first row closest to the whiteboard and the teacher replied, 'Just this once'.

In Aydın, in the district of Germencik in October 2006, researchers interviewing members of the Izmir Romani Association were told that in the local school non-Roman students had been transferred to other schools in the area, and many of the teachers had resigned when the Romani children were introduced to the school in the previous year.

In one appalling incident recorded in Afyon's Şuhut neighbourhood, also in October 2006, the local Izmir Association members told of how the headmaster of the school had become embroiled in a conflict with one of the Romani students (researchers were not told the nature of this conflict), and incited the people in the marketplace to attack the Romani dwellings. As a result, the Romanlar had been forced to move out of Afyon.

A young man from Kağithane in Istanbul said that the previous year he had wanted to attend a private Koran school, after a representative from the school entered the neighbourhood in order to recruit young people. He went to the school to register where he was told that they did not accept Gypsies.

In Şavşat (August 2007), a Lom family related the following case. Some time before one of their daughters had been the highest achieving student at her school but in spite of this the school administration had tried to prevent her from giving the annual student speech at the diploma ceremony, instead awarding this honour to a local doctor's daughter because their daughter was 'Posha' and 'not decent enough'. The family protested and in the end their daughter was allowed to give the speech after all. In the area, the children at school were divided into classes A, B and C, where the children of 'respected' families attended class A, while the 'Posha' children were all grouped into class C.

For Romanlar interviewees in Izmir and Manisa, the attitude of staff in public hospitals made it clear that they did not approach Romani patients as positively as they do to non-Romani patients. The main reason for the differences in the treatments of Romani citizens in public hospitals is their perceived physical differences, according to the interviewees (August 2006). For example, Saniye Hanim, a 40-year old resident of Tepecik Mahallesi in Izmir, attended a public hospital regularly in order to receive treatment for her legs. She stated that whenever she went to the hospital to see the doctor all the staff, including her doctor, spoke to her differently and kept her waiting more than they kept other patients waiting. 'It is not just my being Roma that makes me different, he [the doctor] speaks with a different [negative] tone,' she told researchers.

In Şavşat (August 2007) researchers were told that in hospitals discrimination against the Lom was common. Apparently if the hospital staff knew (it was not explained how they might 'know') patients were 'Posha' then they were made to wait longer than necessary, even if it was an emergency. 'If they don't know you are 'Posha' then you get much better service,' one man explained.

In Izmir's Ikiceşmelik *mahallesi* (August 2006) another man who was undergoing treatment for cancer, asserted that doctors and nurses at the hospital did not treat him in a polite manner; he felt his Romani origins were the main reason for that.

In Kirklarelli (September 2006), a respondent told researchers that 'they [Gypsies]... are usually subjected to discrimination and are excluded in the hospitals on the basis of their "unhygienic" conditions [that is, they were considered "dirty"] and their Romani accents [distinctive in the dropping of the letter "h" at the beginning of words amongst Thracian Romanlar]'.

In 2006 in Thrace, in the Aydoğdu Gypsy quarter, a Romani lady reported that when she came to give birth in the local hospital a year before she was taken to a separate room for 'Gypsy' women.

Struggles over housing, land use and mass evictions

In the Agora neighbourhood of Izmir, a 70-year-old lady explained that she cannot get a house to rent in either her own neighbourhood or in other neighbourhoods as the owners know she is Roma (August 2006). In the small settlement of Tire in the Aegean region of Izmir, Romanlar also spoke about the discrimination landlords and property owners showed towards them as 'Gypsies' (May 2007).

In the Hancepek neighbourhood in Diyarbakir, the local Kurdish residents collected 2,000 signatures on a petition that they presented to the local *muhtar* asking for the 'Gypsies' to be forcibly removed from the area; the *muhtar* in this case refused the petition. In Kadiköy, Istanbul, however, the local *muhtar* in the neighbourhood was behind the collection of signatures on a similar petition, according to respondents there (August 2006).

In the Tevfik Fikret Caddesi in Küçukbakkalköy, demolition was carried out two months before researchers visited the neighbourhood (July 2006), destroying 70 or 80 houses that were home to some 300 children. The demolition programme carried out by the Istanbul Metropolitan Municipality was undertaken with the assistance of the police force. The families received no notification before the event and the bulldozers, assisted by 600 police officers from the special forces, arrived at 5.30 am, waking the inhabitants. Reportedly, the police had told the residents that they had come to carry out cleaning (it was not clear from the interviews exactly what kind of cleaning this was) and asked them to wait in the street. While they were waiting in the street, bulldozers started demolishing the houses with all the property and effects (and the domestic pets in some cases) inside the houses. Some of the inhabitants climbed up onto their roofs in order to stop the destruction of houses, acting as human shields. After some hours of stalemate in this confrontation (sometime around 10.00 am according to the residents researchers spoke to), the police launched tear gas (called 'pepper gas' by the residents) and forcibly began removing people from the houses.

At least one instance of what appears to be the use of demolition to 'punish' an individual or family appears to have taken place in Istanbul in the Kuçukbakkalköy neighbourhood when a family dwelling was demolished even though there existed all the correct documentation to avoid this taking place (during the demolition of July 2006). No explanation for this action was offered at the time but an apology for making a 'mistake' was issued (according to residents interviewed in September 2006).

In Kirklarelli (September 2006) residents gave the example of a fire that broke out on 11 September in the woods close to the Yayla mahallesi, Kırklareli (Çamlık). The inhabitants of the *mahalle* called the fire brigade but there was no response by the firefighters. The inhabitants quenched the blaze themselves. The man who related the event told researchers that the fire crews do not trust their emergency calls because of their Romanlar origins.

This unprecedented action research during 2006–08, led by a person of Romanichal and Irish Traveller heritage, worked closely with the Romanlar, Domlar and Lomlar communities to build confidence and trust in the process of investigating the issues that affect them on a daily basis. The research documented the extent of the prejudices, discrimination and abuse that the Romanlar, Domlar, Lomlar, Gezginler and Göcebe groups in Turkey experience, and demonstrated that the social, economic and cultural position of Gypsies is not merely the same as any other group of poor Turks. Poverty, marginalisation and exclusion are not the causes of these problems but their consequences.

The research produced a great deal of data that will provide a resource for future research for years to come, but more importantly, provided a sound knowledge base for the community self-awareness required to organise for change.

References

Acton, T. and Marsh, A. 2007. *Report on ESRC Research Project Charting the Variety of Aspirations of Romani/Gypsy groups in Turkey (Ref RES-000-22-1652).* ESRC Swindon.

Belton, Brian. 2005. *Questioning Gypsy Identity: Ethnic Narratives in Britain and America.* Walnut Creek, California: Alta Mira Press.

Crowe, David. 1996. *A History of the Gypsies of Eastern Europe and Russia.* London: Palgrave Macmillan.

Greenwich University: <www.gre.ac.uk>; Professor Acton's web page <http://www. gre.ac.uk/schools/humanities/departments/sccs/staff_directory/thomas_acton>.

Gypsy Roma Traveller History Month website: <www.grthm.co.uk>.

Hancock, Ian. 2002. *We Are the Romani People; Ame Sam e Rromane dzene.* Hatfield: University of Hertfordshire Press/Paris: Centre de recherches tsiganes; Professor Hancock's web page <http://radoc.net/>.

Lemon, Alaina. 2000. *Between Two Fires: Gypsy Performance and Romani Memory from Pushkin to Post-Socialism.* New York: Duke University Press.

Marsh A. 2008 '"No Promised Land", History, Historiography and the Origins of the Gypsies'. PhD Thesis, University of Greenwich <http://homepage.mac.com/ adrianrmarsh/Romani_Studies>, password 'Romany'.

Marushiakova, Elena and Popov, Vesselin. 2001. *Gypsies in the Ottoman Empire: a Contribution to the History of the Balkans,* Olga Apostolova [trans.], Donald Kenrick [ed.]. Hatfield: University of Hertfordshire Press/Paris: Centre de Recherches Tsiganes.

Romany and Traveller Family History Society website: <www.rtfhs.org.uk>.

Adrian Marsh was coordinator of the ERRC/hCa/EDROM research project for the programme 'Promoting Romani Rights in Turkey', funded by the European Commission. In 2006–07 he was Researcher in Romani studies at the University of Greenwich, London for the ESRC 'Charting the Variety of Aspirations of Romani Gypsy groups in Turkey' research project, and in 2005–06 was Project Consultant to the British Council/ Ministry of National Education (Turkey) programme 'Developing Social Inclusion in Education for Disadvantaged Children'. He has been a community education worker in the NGO sector (1980–99), and for the Haringey Traveller Education Service in

London (2000–02).

3

Knowing Gypsies

Dr Brian Belton

YMCA George Williams College
London

It is quite a challenge to squeeze into a few pages the ideas and impressions that might constitute knowledge accrued about Gypsies, Travellers and Roma from 30 years of research, while somehow adequately mediating this with the experience and impact of my own, what I have come to call in my own mind, 'Traveller heritage'. So rather than go through a load of rather dry stuff about the pragmatics of my research while seeking to justify this as a 'Gypsy academic' (part of my own identity that I am pretty much fed up with justifying to Gorjer and 'born again Roma') I thought I would provide something about the 'bigger how' – the attitude that has guided my research, as it is that which has dictated, refined and made clear the methodology I have deployed not only in the books about Gypsy and Traveller identity I have written but in the close to 40 books I had published on a range of subjects. It is based on what people say about themselves (what academics might call their 'identity') and others rather than a detached set of theories. But these 'sayings' are more than just statements, mere words uttered, taken out of their context in time and place and reproduced as 'evidence'. What I have tried to do is portray views in what might be thought of as a stream of understanding and insight, and what this seems to give rise to is that what people see themselves to be is, in the main, not a one-dimensional social or ethnic type, but what I have come to think of as 'resultant beings': they point out a range of influences and lineages that are expanded over time and across circumstances. Personal testimonies intersect, diverge and divert, and while there are life stories that portray a constancy of identity, in the main I have found the opposite to be the case.

For instance, in 1974 I was told this story by a man who told me his name was John Warner:

> I was born a Travelling man and it's a full-blooded Romany is what I am. My father was on the road and my grandfather before him going all the way back. All my family is the same. Travelling is in my blood and I could live no other way.

At this point I was a youth and community worker in Glasgow. This was said on my first meeting with John Warner. Eighteen months later I now understood the man to be David Walker. He told me:

> My grandfather was a farmhand and he married my grandmother who was in service in a big house a few miles away. By the time my father and his brothers were born my grandfather was working all over, a day here, a couple of days there. But he was getting work a long way off and that's when the family started to travel. But my dad had gone to school and got work in a factory and rented a place. But when he came back from the war he couldn't get back into that. He just couldn't stand it. So he took to the road. My sister lives in Canada and my brother in Australia. But I kind of took up the work my father did and the road was my life. I have a place near Kidderminster and when I stop work I'll live there.

Things had changed for me and this person. He saw me differently and I certainly understood him more than I did on our first meeting. This is not unusual. We all experience this in our lives to a greater or lesser extent; we change identities even in terms of our own comprehension of who we are over time and according to where we are standing. That for me is why identity, and particularly Gypsy identity, is always complex and in a state of flux. But this said, culture is culture because it changes and not because it stays the same; if it stayed the same it would be congruent with the Nazi view of tradition that proposes stasis/continuity as evidence of superiority.

I suppose this way of understanding the world goes back at least 300 years. We can call the eighteenth century the age of the Enlightenment because it was both a culmination and a new beginning. Fresh currents of thought were wearing down institutionalised traditions. New ideas and new approaches to old institutions were setting the stage for great revolutions to come. One very quick way to conceive this time is to look back to September 1784, when a Berlin magazine, *Berlinische Monatsschrift* (Berlin Monthly) edited by Friedrich

Gedike and Johann Erich Biester, invited several German intellectuals to answer the question 'Was ist Aufklärung?' (*What is Enlightenment?*). They included the philosopher Immanuel Kant who, in December of that same year, rose to the challenge with a vigour and clarity not always evident in his lengthier works. His essay included the following lines:

> Enlightenment is man's emergence from his self-incurred immaturity. Immaturity is the inability to use one's own understanding without direction from another. This immaturity is self-incurred if its cause is not lack of understanding, but lack of resolve and courage to use it without another's guidance. *Sapere aude!* Dare to know! That is the motto of Enlightenment.

This is about going to the direct source of knowledge by one's own observations and not relying on 'traditional' views or conventional thought. In the *Critique of Pure Reason,* which had been published three years earlier and established his reputation throughout Europe, Kant had sought to reconcile the two dominant schools of modernist philosophy – the British empiricist approach of Bacon, Locke and Hume (who held that knowledge was the product of experience and experiment, and thus subject to amendment) and the continental rationalism exemplified by Descartes and Spinoza, which maintained that certainty could be achieved by inferential reasoning from first principles ('I think therefore I am'). What these traditions had in common was far more important than what divided them, and by incorporating elements from both, Kant was able to demolish the pretensions of religion to superior knowledge or understanding. 'The critical path alone is still open,' he announced after almost 700 pages, having cleared away the metaphysical obstacles:

> If the reader has had the courtesy and patience to accompany me along this path, he may now judge for himself whether, if he cares to lend his aid in making this path into a high-road, it may not be possible to achieve before the end of the present century what many centuries have not been able to accomplish; namely, to secure for human reason complete satisfaction in regard to that with which it has all along so eagerly occupied itself, though hitherto in vain.

This 'way' or path that Kant offered was, as Foucault would argue in the latter part of the twentieth century, not a theory or a doctrine or even a permanent body of knowledge that is accumulating; it has to be conceived as an attitude, an ethos, a philosophical life in which the critique of what we are is at one and the same time the historical analysis of the limits that are imposed on us and an experiment with the possibility of going beyond them. As such the historical period that we call 'the Enlightenment' did not give rise to an ideology but asked human beings to develop an attitude, a presumption that certain truths about humankind, society and the natural world could be perceived, whether through deduction or observation, and that the discovery of these truths would transform the quality of life and that would occur by the questioning of ideas and what others would call 'reality' or 'facts'. This was, to a certain extent, stylised in Marxist dialectic; this is something more than mere 'discourse', it is a kind of promise to 'work with and develop ideas'.

The knowledge of self and identity cannot be an exception to this standard and, as such, whatever you might conceive or believe Gypsy identity to be, the only sure thing that can be said about it is, like everything else, it is ever-changing as ideas and people themselves adapt to, develop and incorporate their environment. The notion of a permanent and unchanging Gypsy identity is, as such, related much more to the thinking of the 'dark ages' than it is to post-enlightened thought; it is in fact regressive.

The power of the Enlightenment and the thought that came out of it was not so much in what was preached as in the passion of the preacher and the beneficial effects of the sermon. What distinguished the Enlightenment, above all, was its determination to subject all received opinions to the test of reason, to apply this test especially to views on human behaviour, ethical and political theory, and to extract from the knowledge won through this process whatever could be useful in improving the lot of humanity.

All this might be summed up in the words of Eldridge Cleaver, former Black Panther and civil rights activist: 'Too much agreement kills the chat!'

The above might be seen as the shortcut to my own motivation to understand something of Gypsy identity.

I was brought up, like many of my generation born just a few years after the Second World War, within the shadow of the Holocaust. It horrified me as a child and especially as a person with links to a particular group that were consigned to the concentration camps of Europe; it could have been me – it still might be. It was whilst I was in Canada in the early 1970s that I met Kwame Ture (Stokeley Carmichael) and it was through his encouragement that I started to look at what Ashley Montagu called 'Man's Most Dangerous Myth' – the idea of race. I resolved to *discover the truths* about this phenomenon in order to do something, perhaps just a little, to *transform the quality of life*.

I did this in the ways most accessible to me as a naive investigator – examination of my own experience and the exploration of the experience of others. But crucially the process is one of constant questioning of my own taken-for-granted assumptions and of what I hear from other people. I think a clue about this attitude came up in a recent radio interview I did with BBC Radio Three in association with Radio Prague:

> How many books written on Gypsies have been full of people writing down what Gypsies have told them? An oral culture – an intensely oral culture – talking to an intensely written culture. Why should anybody think that this material will constitute something called the truth? Why do you think that? But it's in the library, it's on the shelf, and that's what informs people. It's an empire of written words. It's an empire of writing that exists separately from people like my dad. Here's a man whose mum was a Gypsy, he came from a society of traditional Gypsies going back hundreds of years, and yet he will respond to much of this material by saying, 'This is a load of bollocks'. But, you see, there's no one going to publish that.

> One thing about my dad was that he could tell anyone anything. Other people would say that's because he was a Gypsy, a rascally rogue. He was a terrible liar, and he was able to tell someone something about themselves or somebody else or the world, and they'd totally believe it. He had a gift to do it, and he got a buzz out of it. You know, a storyteller can manipulate the person they're telling the story to. They learn to do it quite young – I don't think it's something you pick up when you're 48. You know, I was brought up to tell lies. We were told constantly not to tell that person the truth – don't tell the authorities the truth, just tell them what they need to know. We had it drummed into us, and I don't think I'm alone in that. In fact I know I'm not. You tell them stories. You find out what clicks into people's minds and you tell them the story they want to hear. A lot of Gypsies are good at that … A lot of people are good at that.

My father has a strong Gypsy heritage. His father's mother was also a Gypsy of Kent. He witnessed his grandmother cremated by her family in a glass coffin in her caravan at the stroke of midnight. It had an impact on him. He is also more than this but this is much of him: his Gypsiness is complex – it is something he lives rather than explains.

My perception of him might sound quite cynical, but fighting is, to a certain extent, one type of ultimate realism, be this of the bare-knuckle variety or the type the struggle for enlightenment provokes – it was Goethe (the writer and philosopher born smack in the middle of the Enlightenment in the Germany of 1749) who said, 'Sometimes, in order to tell the truth, we must defy the truth…'.

That is the fight – to defy the given truth by questioning it – be this the truth about Gypsies, ethnicity or anything else. Being a Gypsy, I think, involves me in this fight; for me not to accept, to be sceptical, is part my Gypsy identity: this is a form of 'travelling' – the refusal to just 'stay in one place' because someone else (usually a Gorjer) thinks I should. But as Goethe also had it: 'Rob a man of his most precious lie and he will want to kill you'.

However, do we have some responsibility – the Enlightenment itself has deeper roots than the usually understood European heritage. Students of Enlightenment thought have often been accused of 'eurocentrism' but the seeds of the way of thinking I have discussed can be found in much older Arab and Islamic thought, as works like *The Travels of Ibn Battuta* (1952) indicate (see also *Ibn Khaldun's Science of Human Culture,* 1996). This 'ancestry of thought' indicates that thinking about Gypsies (and perhaps identity in general) must come from a global ('oceanic') perspective. The European Enlightenment might be thought of as a relatively convenient coalition of ideas in time that makes referencing and orientation more immediate and/or meaning more discernible. The age and place might be thought of more as a turnpike on which ideas coagulated to inspire a continuing intellectual movement than the definitive source of the same.

The work of Spencer Wells (*The Journey of Man* [2003] and *Deep Ancestry* [2006]) demonstrates the common origin of humanity and how our shared history is premised in the urge or need to move, migrate, to travel. This lineage shows humanity, as a species, to be insatiably curious and eager to seek beyond the prospect they can at any one time perceive; horizons, geographical, physical, spiritual or intellectual, seem to draw us towards and beyond them. The broad expanse of humanity seems to be in a 'journey of oneness': we are all 'Travellers'. This resonates with the Islamic notion of *Ummah*. Differences, such as language or ritual for instance, come to be understood as peripheral artefacts that are transitional and epiphenomenal, continually changing cultural tools of a dozen or so generations. Breathing life into these relics in terms of the totality of human existence feels more divisive than creative and appears to generate what Stuart Hall has called *weak power* as we take up our prescribed racial and ethnic categories that were first devised not by our 'ancestors' but by those who had a stake in enslaving and exploiting particular economic groups at the conception of capitalism.

Enlightenment thought, with its emphasis on questioning and doubt, represented an elaboration of the insight that we can always know more, which is another way of saying that we cannot know all. People, men and women, pose infinite questions and the limits on perceptive apparatus alone (as Descartes began to discover in his *Discourse on Method* as early as 1637) provide grounds for doubt. In this spirit, education can be thought of as a train, steaming along a railway of learning, stopping at stations of knowledge, on the way to a destination of complete understanding that can never be reached.

For all this, Gorjer and self-identifying Romani (many of whom I have not known from Adam) have told me where I come from ('India') or where I belong ('in a caravan'/'on a site'). The same people have told me I do or do not act/live/smell/walk/talk/sound/drink/look/write/eat/smoke/dress/dance/ make love like a Gypsy. I have been told I can't be a Gypsy unless I live (at least some of the time) in a caravan. I have been told I can't call myself a 'Gypsy' (at different times I've been told I should be 'Romani', 'Roma' or 'Traveller'). Latterly I have been told by 'expert Gypsies' that I shouldn't ask if Gypsies are an ethnicity. These 'tellers', interpreters of how I should be as a Gypsy, all 'know' me without knowing me. They also know 'how' I should be and often they say they know how I 'feel'. Some of them have qualifications and/ or research to back up their contentions, others relate to their 'instincts' and/ or their experiences of others 'like me' to underwrite their conclusions. I have been told that a 'Gypsy will always recognise another Gypsy'. But when I once asked if a Gypsy from Turkestan might recognise a Gypsy from Luxembourg I was told not to be stupid.

All this stuff appears to be built on the sands of emotional reactions and perhaps insecurities. Looking for a place for and a justification of self in a time of doubt about relationships, a locale of family and social cohesion in a world that seems often to have few anchors or refuges, is understandable. We are desperate to 'belong' and we identify (build identity with) others who seek similar ports in the storms of life. However, this search for affinity also necessarily entails identification of the 'other'; in the process of identifying who's 'in', we simultaneously distinguish who's 'out'. This involves a continuing process of discrimination.

As such, the impassioned promotion by Zionistic Gypsies of an archaic dialect or resurrected 'blood language', the tortured 'Gypsiologists' protesting for the preservation of sets of recorded and observed 'traditions', 'customs', 'rites' and habitats in the interests of preserving some imagined Gypsy equivalent of 'Volk', or the British National Party (BNP) assessing 'Saxon heritage' and 'genetic Britishness' all feel to me like different results of a toss of the same coin, flicked in the rancid atmosphere of a cattle truck en route to the means of discrimination and prejudice; the abode of 'otherness'.

But Gypsy or no, those tutored by the scribblings and rants of distracted seekers of the 'noble savage' within the British rural idyll cannot 'know' me in some hygienic way. Many years ago I attended an education conference. I was introduced to a group of people thus: 'This is Brian. He's a Traveller from East London.' The first question I was asked was, 'Have you got a job?' I smiled and said that I had a job. The response was almost immediate: 'Oh well done!' Someone else asked, 'Do you read crystal balls? The other year we had Gypsies who did that.' I said I didn't have my crystal ball with me but I could read palms. I spent the next 40 minutes or so indulging a swiftly formed queue. My attempt at irony had backfired and I politely played the part expected of me.

This experience and others like it, alongside reading the body of literature from trash novels to the work of acclaimed anthropologists that similarly conjures up identity via 'Gypsy ways', caused me to decide that I, as a Gypsy, would be no-one's itinerant Bilbo Baggins, nor would I accept the garb of Dracula's coachman or anything in between. I will not be placed on a categorical reservation nor will I accept my allotted place on a hard-cored bantustan; I no more 'belong' on a site or in a caravan (metaphoric or otherwise) than I do in a bender tent or a modern Native American 'belongs' in a wigwam! I will not be labelled as representative of some 'type' cobbled together on foundations of legend, myth and the rambling, insane taxonomies of Victorian romantics trapped in the psychic aftershock of an age of fevered nationalism. I am essentially not 'other'; I am wholly 'of' but, as the Enlightenment revealed, within that I am quintessentially exceptional and distinctive; that is what I have in common with you and everyone else. We are all bound together by our common uniqueness. Recognising and living (and sometimes doubting) that is part of *my* Gypsy identity.

Maybe it is something to do with my Gypsy identity, but all my life (with one or two exceptions – see above) I have refused to remain in the same place; to stay where I have been put. Much of what I have been told is the truth I have doubted, probably because some person has insisted that their words (that are usually written down somewhere) linked together make a thing called 'truth'. This feels like a lie because I have found that truth is hardly ever in the telling as it appears to be something constantly in the process of being made; we tend to *move* towards it, but in order to find it, we need to keep on looking for it, we are obliged to *travel*. This same discovery has been made by individuals and groups ever since (and probably before) the Enlightenment. The code of the Black Panthers was to 'question everything'. They also found that white supremacist society did not have the capacity to liberate black people and as such communities would need to take responsibility for their own emancipation (*movement* from 'unfreedom' to liberation, in order to survive they could not *stay in the same place* even though the white-controlled authorities wanted them to).

Kant's essay, written 225 years ago, included a look at the obstacles to enlightenment and the prerequisites needed for people to enlighten themselves. For Kant, church and state paternalism needed to be swept aside so conditions might be set in place for people to be free to use their own intellect. As such, Immanuel might be thought of as the first Panther! He provides an enduring message for 'unfree' communities in general but for Gypsies in particular he demonstrates that we cannot rely on Gorjer writing and words for truth or liberty; these are things we need to create for ourselves by our continued resolve to *travel* – to move towards the horizon of our personal and collective Enlightenment. This might entail the need to cease to be a 'type' (reject externally generated categories) that others excavate knowledge from for delivery in contexts that hardly any of us have access to and so cannot add to, refine, question or deny (as subjects). It may mean we can begin to assertively define ourselves and our context; perhaps 'they' have looked at 'us' long enough (made us objects). Maybe the time has come for 'us' to investigate 'them'. Herein lies the potential to question and perhaps desist from emulating the whole hideous and outlandish pursuit of generating apparently immutable biological or dispositional human dichotomies, racial/ethnic/cultural categories, out of the effects of social inequality and economic exploitation. This is a nasty and inhumane legacy of the primal eugenicists who sought to establish grounds for racial supremacism that in effect worked to preserve the economic hegemony of existing elites.

There is a twinkling light of logic on the boundaries of conception that suggests that there is no 'them' and 'us', no controllers or controlled, only 'we'. Of course, the current controllers will not want to move towards that glimmer. They will even recruit some of the controlled (in the slave/colonial context 'the native') by trick, bribe or indoctrination, to preserve the status quo, promote difference and discord (language is an excellent and traditional vehicle for this), and camouflage commonality and solidarity, helping to set a course away from this beam that might increase enlightenment.

The Black Panthers' scepticism and insistence on independence of thought, I believe, made them Enlightenment thinkers. One of their number, the still exiled Assata Shakur, maybe gives us some incentive to review our own commitment to personal enlightenment – to look towards our personal and community horizons and travel:

I am only one woman. I own no TV stations, or radio stations or newspapers. But I feel that people need to be educated as to what is going on, and to understand the connection between the news media, white-run institutions and the instruments of repression. All I have is my voice, my spirit and the will to tell the truth. But I sincerely ask those of you ... those of you in the progressive media, those who struggle in the corrupt educational institutions, those of you who believe in truth, freedom, let people know what is happening. We have no voice, so you must be the voice of the voiceless.

4

The construction of the history of the Roma in the 'Great Land' (Russia): notions of Roma history and identity in Imperial, Soviet and post-Soviet Russia

Valdemar Kalinin

There is a remarkable continuity in Roma identity between the pre-Soviet era of the Russian Empire, the Soviet era, and the post-Soviet era that has been remarked on both by myself and by Alaina Lemon (2000). Research in the archives of the former Russia and Soviet Union enable us to explore the reasons for this by seeking for the answers given by Soviet scholars to the following questions.

- How was it possible that such mental strength or common consciousness developed among the Roma to enable them to retain their identity as a nationality with very little assistance from State institutions such as schools, the army and the judicial systems, none of which they controlled?
- The strong Romani customary code, which is very similar among many groups of Roma, might give reason to presume that Roma once lived in a state as a separate caste. How did Roma in Russia speculate as to where and when?
- Why is it that other former nomadic nations whose migrations took place further back in history accept common historical accounts of their migration routes and their historic motherland – Turks, American Indians, Bulgarians, Kyrgyz, Hungarians, Yakuts, Eskimos – but many Roma still do not accept India as their motherland?
- How has the fall of the Iron Curtain enabled new sources and archives to emerge and researchers from Eastern Europe to interact with researchers from Western Europe to re-examine the history and origins of Roma?

On the eve of the 1917 October Revolution the Russian Empire was a huge entity. It was diverse in landscape and population, especially after it incorporated eastern Poland (in 1796) and Finland (in 1810) into its realm. Yet there were many problems threatening to tear the Empire apart from within. There was an ever-widening gap between the Russian aristocracy and the oppressed peasants who were literally starving to death. This gap between rich and poor cut across all in society, including the Roma. There was, furthermore, a big difference between the Russian Urban Roma – the *Foritka Roma* – and the nomadic Roma. The first group often intermarried with the Russian gentry and were able to educate their children in *Gymnasiums*. Urban Roma were represented in 28 different professions including doctors and pharmacists; by contrast, the nomadic group lived in tents and were usually illiterate.

The Urban Roma had set up musical groups and choirs. They had also founded unions with the aim of caring for elderly Roma who had performed for a number of years in these music associations. These Roma spoke Greek and French, and knew some Latin, but often they had a poor command of Romanes, usually just enough to perform in the language.

The nomadic Roma – *Shatritka Roma*, or 'tent-dwelling Roma' – roamed in camps around towns and cities and preserved their untamed modes of dancing and high-pitched singing. Their first language was invariably Romanes.

Russian Roma called themselves *Ruska* or *Rasejska Roma* (Russian), while other Romani ethnic tribes called them *Xhaladytka* (or 'soldier') *Roma*. Among Russian Roma themselves, this appellation has a derogatory edge (Kalinin, 2005).

Russian Roma called all other Romani groups (Lovari, Sinti, Chuxny, Vlaxi) 'Pharaohs' (or Pharaoh people), and the literature and the newspapers of the twentieth century would refer to all Roma as 'Pharaoh's Tribe'. This referenced the theory that the Roma went through Egyptian slavery on their migration from India until crusaders set them free in the eleventh century.

The first justification of the Indian origin of the Roma was propounded in nineteenth-century Russia by a lecturer at Vilnius University, the prominent historian of the Lithuania-Poland region, Tadeusz (Theodore) Narbutt (1784–1864). A Pole by nationality, Narbutt published *A Historical Sketch of the Gypsy People* first in Polish in 1830 and then in Russian in 1850. In it, clearly drawing on Grellmann (1783), he states that all Roma originate from a caste in India, the remnant of which vanished after the Roma's exodus from the land due to population increases amongst other castes. Narbutt was strongly opposed to the suggestion that the invasion of Genghis Khan had stimulated the Roma exodus: he postulated that, by the time of the invasion, Roma had already been recorded in the Byzantine Empire.

In the later Russian Empire and its successor, the Soviet state, it was taken for granted that the origin of Gypsies (Roma) was Indian. The Slavic and Baltic languages have more in common with Sanskrit than the Germanic and Romance languages and therefore the people living there feel strongly their affiliation with India. The question was posed, 'Why did the Roma people leave a land as pleasant as India?' Most scholars of the time came to accept that the Roma originated from India and they sought to confirm the hypothesis that ancestors of the Roma originated from the 'Jats' and/or 'Nats' tribe/caste. It was believed that the Nats travelled as horse dealers and musicians, accompanying the Indian armies during their military campaigns. The earliest widely available source on Romani history is the 1848 *Directorial Encyclopaedic Dictionary* of St Petersburg where it is mooted that all Roma came from Hungary and Moldava, not from Egypt. The next academic book which touches on the issue is the *Russian Encyclopaedic Dictionary* (Vol. 15) published in 1873. It puts forward a theory that 'proto-Roma' were known as the 'Karachi' who roamed around Persia and have been recorded since the fifth century. It also states that:

> These people came to Europe during the X–XI centuries and remained in Asia Minor, Syria and Egypt, where they left their representatives in clans like the Helebi, Ghagar, Nawar, Kurbat and Tzingani. The Roma are likely to originate from Dzats (Jats) or, as E Trump states, they are from the Bhangi tribe which was diluted and disappeared during a move from Sind into Beluchistan and Persia.

The *Great Encyclopaedia of the Russian Empire* (1909) concluded that:

> Gypsies are a nomadic tribe of obscure origin who came from India, and the closest ethnic groups to them are Jats and Nat[s].

The Soviet state recognised the Roma as a national minority with the right to be educated in their native language, Romanes, in 1925. The Romani population numbered 62,300 in those days and was divided into two groups: local Roma and foreign Roma. The local Roma were made up of northern and southern Russian Roma, Ukrainian and Crimean Roma, and Luli Roma from Central Asia. All the rest, including the Kalderari, Lovari, Lithuanian/Latvian, Polish, Sinti, Vlax and other Romani representatives were considered foreign Roma.

Great efforts were made by the nascent Roma intelligentsia to create a Romani literary language consistent with Russian orthography. It was based on the lexicon common to northern and southern Russian Romani dialects.

The high point of the Romani Enlightenment occured during 1925–38 when Romani schools, crèches and colleges were opened up to serve the needs of the tillers of the Romani *kolkhozes* (collective farms) and the Romani cartels (cooperatives).

The famous Indian poet Rabindranath Tagore visited the Soviet Union in 1930. He met poets, writers and government workers of Romani origin; it was he who inspired the Romani intellectuals and the Soviet authorities to move forward with Romani art and culture (according to the archives of Nikolai Pankov, no date). Tagore was presented with a special set of five books of Romani literature that were designed to be used in schools. He took the floor as a poet, philosopher and philologist and his impact on the public opinion of the Romani–Indian link was great.

The Indian origin of the Roma was by now undisputed. It was thus that the first Romani state theatre, *Studio Romen*, inaugurated in December 1931, came to be called the Indian Theatre-Studio of the Romani Art. As a matter of fact, new personal names of Indian origin came into use among the Roma during this period, such as Ganga, Inda, Indira, Rada and Radz.

Lev Gumilev (1912–92) was a controversial Soviet-Russian 'racial scientist', prominent geographer, poet, martyr of the Red Regime, and child of two outstanding Russian poets (his mother was the prominent poet Anna Akhmatova and his father was avant-garde poet Nikolaj Gumilev, executed by Cheka in 1921). Gumilev was amazed at how Roma, having been separated from their motherland India, had managed to preserve their language, culture and ethnic identity. Gumilev himself spent more than 15 years in a Gulag where he mastered Chinese, Hindi and Turkish. Gumilev (1978, 1990) argued that 'ancestors of the Roma belonged to the lowest caste Doma and they left India during the Rajput revolution in the [seventh] century'. He offered the hypothesis that ancestors of the Roma escaped India not as one group, but gradually. The Roma as we know them took shape as a nation outside India, after the exodus and after the Rajput revolution inspired by the philosopher Kumarila (sixth century AD) and later his successor Sankara (788–820), who started to doubt Buddhist teachings. They founded their own philosophic doctrines based on the call to turn back to true Brahmanism (Gumilev, 1990). They inspired Rajputs to seize an opportunity to take sabres to crush the Guptas Empire. As a result the caste system was reconstructed. All those people who opposed this revolution found themselves placed in the low caste, touchable. For the untouchables, however, their yet lower status made life unbearable and they began to perceive a risk that they might be annihilated. Gumilev (1990) argued that representatives of low castes therefore started to flee India, later emerging in Central Asia, still in the Near East: they were afterwards traced to Europe and Russia.

The first census taken in the Soviet state in 1926 counted 61,299 Gypsies, according to the *Great Soviet Encyclopedia*, (1934, Vol. 60). This publication also stated that 'the Roma could have left India in the tenth century and they moved westward by two routes: first, alongside the Persian bay; second, through inner Persia'. The book also condemns the last decree by Tsar Nicholas II in 1903 which declared an unconditional ban on the right of Gypsies to roam, and points out that the October Revolution changed the situation for Gypsies entirely. In 1926, 1928 and 1932 respectively the Soviet state issued the following laws/decrees:

- to settle the Roma by supplying them with land and finance
- to organise and support Romani cartels (cooperatives)
- to improve the level of culture through Romani schools/institutions and media.

The next *Great Soviet Encyclopaedia* (1957) stated that 'the Roma had to leave India for historical reasons'. The final edition of the *Great Soviet Encyclopedia* (1978) enumerated the Gypsies in the USSR according to the census taken in 1970, and quoted the by now established opinion of world science, which allowed them to declare the Indian origin of Roma. It is also mentioned that Gypsies were formed 'as a nationality' after the exodus from India at the end of first millennium. It praised the powerful decree 'On Reconciling Vagrant Gypsies to Labour' in which Khrushchev reversed Stalin's earlier policy of voluntary rather than forced settlement as a good step for Gypsies, to help them transfer themselves to a sedentary and a working way of life.

In the last census taken during the Soviet era, Roma in Russia numbered 209,000 (*Great Soviet Encyclopedia*, 1979). The most recent edition of the *Great Russian Encyclopedia* (2006, Vol. 57: 485–94) states that, 'ancestors of the Roma were nomadic musicians who used to entertain counts (Rajs) and who looked after the domestic needs of their palaces. Their social castes are unknown'.

The author of this entry in the encyclopedia, however, challenges earlier accounts by arguing that the Roma could not have originally belonged to a low caste, but that after the Muslim invasion of India in the tenth century the usual way of life was disrupted. The invaders were not interested in Gypsy music and dancing. Other activities and jobs had been monopolised by that time by other castes and there was no business for the ancestors of the Roma. They started to leave India in groups and were joined by other bands of exiles, from whom the Roma may have learnt blacksmithing and other crafts.

This contrasts with Soviet-era views, such as those that appeared in the *Ukrainian Soviet Encyclopedia* (1964, Vol. 16: 35–6) that stated that it is entirely accepted that 'Gypsies originated from Western-Northern India from the nomadic nations who belonged to the low castes'. They specify that the Roma started to leave India due to the Muslim invasion.

In 1970 researchers in Czechoslovakia commenced thorough research into Romani genetic history, concluding that the Roma are much closer to Indians than their national compatriots, as reported in the *Slovakian Encyclopedia* (1977, Vol. 1: 320–2). In this respect, the recent findings about the genetic history of the Roma by Luba Kalaydjieva (Chaix et al., 2004) confirmed and greatly extended the conclusions of the Czech researchers. The Czech scientists' Soviet colleagues, however, did not altogether approve of their findings, dismissing them as racially motivated, but the results of the research were not criticised officially.

During the period when the Soviet Union was collapsing, the *Great Encyclopedic Dictionary* (1991, Vol.2: 620–1) entry on 'Gypsies' suggested that they are an ethnically united people having lived in many countries, including the USSR, self-ascribed as 'Rom' and whose ancestors came from India at the end of first millennium. It suggests 'that Gypsies originated in India, with many migrating to Russia by way of Germany and Poland during the eighteenth century after suffering persecution there'.

All recent brief academic accounts echo the *Great Russian Encyclopedia* in referring to Gypsies as having 'ethnic commonality', which means that the community takes its shape from different ethnic representatives who live in many countries of the world and whose ancestors came from India at the end of the first millennium, but the scholars tend to stop short of defining Gypsies as one nation. There were 262,000 Gypsies present in the USSR in 1989, compared to 153,000 in Russia in 2003. The 2006 census showed 181,000 Gypsies in Russia.

A reader of this paper may at this point be wondering how the official records reflect the date at which Roma arrived in Russia. The encyclopedias and dictionaries mentioned above declare that Gypsies came to Russia in the fifteenth and sixteenth centuries from Poland. Some contemporary scholars, however, including N. Bessonov (via personal correspondence), assert that the first Gypsy immigrants arrived in the Russian Empire during the reign of Peter the Great at the beginning of the eighteenth century, since the first official Russian document on Gypsies appeared as late as 1731 in Tobolsk, Siberia.

The poet Yefim Druts (who was a well-known researcher of Romani folklore) wrote together with Alexander Gessler (1990: 13–15) that 'ancestors of the Roma came from [the] untouchable caste Doma. The Doma were a … tribe united by ethnicity and language'. They also proposed that it took uncounted years for Romanies to become a nation. Both spent a significant portion of time living amongst the Roma.

The Moscow-based scholar and educationalist Marijanna Smirnova-Seslavinskaya defended her doctorate entitled 'Ethnic/Social Sources of Culture of the Russian Roma' (2006). She and her husband, the prolific writer and scholar Georgi Tsvetkov, carried out a thorough investigation of proto-Romani history based on the Indian sources in cooperation with current Indologists. Smirnova-Seslavinskaya reported at the Ukrainian Romani Conference (Kiev, June 2008) that the results of anthropological and cultural investigation indicate that on a genetic level the Indian ancestry of the Roma is a result of contacts between the local proto-Aryan tribes under the generic name Dom (Domba-Lambadi), and Aryan tribes. The main Aryan group derived from the Iranian Scythians or Saks (Shaks). This process began around 2000 BC and continued until the sixth century AD. Analysis of social and cultural aspects of the Romani people, argued Smirnova-Seslavinskaya and Tsvetkov show that the nomadic Romani household is closely linked to the cattle-breeding tribes of Pashto and Beluch. The principles of the culture and social organisation of Roma 'romanipen' are very close to the Pashto notion of 'pashtonvali'. These scholars put forward their hypothesis that the proto-Roma took shape as a nation alongside other nations in a part of north-western India, 'Kohistan, inhabited by Pashto and Rajputs'. Some groups of the proto-Roma, they posited, were involved in trading, metalwork, weaving, carpentry, fortune-telling, dancing and musical performance. Due to their forced removal to the Byzantine Empire these ancestors of the Roma lost their land and their traditional roles as cattle breeders. Smirnova-Seslavinskya and Tsvetkov suggest that this took place between sixth and eighth centuries before they were recorded in the Byzantine Empire chronicles. They assume that the ancestors of the Roma were deported by Arabs in the sixth century and might be further linked to the history of the Zotts. Smirnova-Seslavinskaya and Tsvetkov thus neatly show that Russian *gaje* scholars can compete with the worst of Western scholars in producing speculative unscientific rubbish on the flimsiest of evidence.

A small group of equally speculative scholars led by the Ukrainian academic Dr Viktor Kandyba (2002) proposed that the Roma entered India (Punjab) as an ancient tribe known as the Chingani (Chanchaar) during the freezing of the climate in the nineteenth and eighteenth centuries BC. They originally lived near the Azov sea. Later, some of their ancestors supposedly came back to the former Russian Empire in the area of Central Asia where they were called Luri (Luli). The next wave of Chingani (Shaigani) returned from India in the sixth century AD and settled in the lands of Uristan (Caucasus) where they were given the name Bosha Karachi. The next wave of them returned to their historical motherland, the Russian Empire, in the seventh century AD where they acclimatised to their new surroundings, ranging from the Azov Sea area as far as the lands bordering the Danube.

There were two common opinions in the Soviet era regarding the Romani way of life through history. Firstly, it was presented at the romantic-poetic level; secondly, it was interpreted as a survival culture in which the seed of a wild way of life was seen. The Russian Empire's governmental acts called upon Russians to root out this survival-centric culture. Vadim Toropov, who is considered an expert on the Crimean Roma, wrote in correspondence to me that by 1994 two opinions had taken shape in Russia: firstly, that the Roma left India around AD 420, long before the Arabs went to the Indian peninsula; secondly, due to the lack of Arabian borrowed words present in Romanes, another hypothesis was suggested – that the Roma left India around AD 1000 and were later converted to Christianity in Armenia around the eleventh century, evidence for this being quite a few borrowings from Armenian church language: for example, *Patradi* (Easter), *ghok* (incense), and *trushul* (cross) amongst others.

Dr Nadezhda Demeter and Nicolai Bessonov (Demeter et al., 2006: 11–15) wrote that a tribe of musicians could have made up the core of the immigrants from India and that those tribes did not leave their motherland once but gradually over a period of two centuries. Even at this late date Nicolai Bessonov held fast to the now wholly discredited view that the only reliable document from the past history of the Roma is the story written down by the Persian poet Firdausi in the ninth century, five centuries after the event described. Bessonov wrote to me that after Soviet power abated there emerged a desire to enhance the standing of the Roma's ancestors. The numerous Romani leaders/presidents felt very uncomfortable that their forefathers had belonged to a low caste and that they had been oppressed and enslaved in the more distant past in Romania prior to 1856. These Romani presidents (or self-appointed barons), he argued, started to compete with Western scholars to raise the status of proto-Roma to an alternative caste. In so doing they were inspired by the late Romani linguist Jan Kochanowski (real name Ivan Petrov, 1920–2007) who embarked on a historical re-evaluation that enhanced Romani social status. The archives of Nikolai Pankov show he drew on earlier physical anthropology of Romani people and compared them with those of the military Kshatriya caste, thereby concluding that Roma were descended from the Kshatriya.

Nikolai Pankov (1895–1959) was a pioneer in Romani education and a prominent poet and translator. He tried hard to cool Jan Kochanowski on the subject of the Roma's links to the high caste Kshatriya as well as on the introduction of new words into the Romani language. This fascinating correspondence suggests that Jan Kochanowski was speculatively linking the

Roma and himself not only to the ancient high caste Rajputs but also to high-ranked Soviet officers and generals, including the famous Soviet Marshal Frunze who probably had no link whatsoever with the Roma since the accepted history is that he was of Russian noble origin.

The well-known Romani director, actor and dramatist Professor Georgiy Zhemchuzny of Moscow Theatre Romen demonstrates (in personal correspondence) that he considers the Roma to be eternal nomads whose ancestors once came to India at a distant stage of history: they remained there for a while, before departing to save their lives or to seek better conditions elsewhere. This is not only his opinion: Zhemchuzny and other actors from the Theatre Romen staged their plays in India for seven months, travelling around the country and meeting different representatives who are sometimes referred to as being related to Roma, including Banjara and Bede. They state that the dance-based and performance elements of Romani stage craft have nothing to do with any equivalent in the Indian nations. Such core aspects of Romani performance are more like those typically found among performers from Iranian and Kurdish backgrounds.

I also corresponded with historians from Russia, Belarus and Ukraine (including Miledy Bunto) who speculated that the Roma's ancestors had their roots in ancient Siginnes, a region mentioned in Homer's *Odyssey*. In due time, waves of different immigrants from India joined them, thus creating the Roma as we know them today. Bunto himself, who claims expertise on ancient Slavic/Baltic history, hypothesised that ancestors of the Roma were among the Scythians/Saks invaders who are credited with being the first to tame horses. They are said to have come to India in the fifth century BC. He suggests the Scythian way of life shows many similarities to that of the Roma, including their grooming of horses, attitude to guard dogs, use of highly mobile domestic facilities and in the clothing of women. In addition, the social structure of the Scythian clan was comparable to that of the Roma (the status of a tribe would be related to the number of tents possessed). He suggests genetic research strengthens the hypothesis that the men were taken as horse dealers and musicians into Persia by Arabs where they remained in the long term and intermarried with local women.

Despite some of the wilder speculations listed above, a scholarly consensus emerged in the Soviet Union and has persisted in post-Soviet Russia that the Roma were nomadic herdsmen and musicians in India who could have left the land in waves due to radical change in the life of the region at some stage of time. Such a body of knowledge was enough to underwrite the national self-consciousness of the educated Roma as they took their place in Soviet and Russian society. It is not unique that we do not know exactly how the Roma as a nation took shape: many other nations lack specific knowledge of their origins. Basques, Georgians, Celts and especially Cossacks may be included in this judgment. We can also witness that a new nation has been formed in our time called Krimchaki (Crimeans).

Finally, we know that some Indians, musicians and craftsmen were also resettled by Persians and Arabs in the plains and marshes of Mesopotamia, then known as Zottistan (Kenrick, 2004). This may have been when the proto-Roma took shape as a nation with a distinct Romani consciousness, its people living together in a relatively self-governed framework that could have made them assess themselves as a separate nation in the context of the other, different nations surrounding them. Invasions and raids by Persians (third century) and later incursions of Arabs into India (647–825) as well as the Rajput revolution could have persuaded the ancestors of the Roma to leave Sind and Punjab. I agree with the prevalent opinion of Roma from Belarus and the Baltic states that there might be more information about Roma in countries like Afghanistan, Iran, Turkey, Armenia and Iraq or even in the archives of Arab states. It is inevitable that the transition of Roma through their lands would have been documented in some way. However, due to political factors, such as the threat of land reclamation, it is impossible to have access to these archives. The process of how a nation/ethnic group takes shape is a long-term historical phenomenon, to which one cannot apply scientific measurements, and it is beyond man's reach, his feelings and observance.

References

Belarus Encyclopedia. 2003. State Publishing House, Minsk. Vol. 17. pp. 140–1.

Bunto, M. 'King Radziwill, Great Jacob Power'. *Respublika* dated 28 June 2008. Minsk. p. 10.

Demeter, N., Bessonov, N. and Kutenkov, V. 2006. *History of Roma*. Private, Voronezh. pp. 11–15.

Directorial Encyclopaedic Dictionary. 1848. St Petersburg.

Druts, Yefim, Druts, E. and Gessler, A. *Gypsies*. 1990. Private, Moscow. pp. 13–15.

Great Encyclopaedia of the Russian Empire (Bolshaya Entsyklopedia Rossiskoy Imperii). 1909. Vol. 19. pp. 759–60.

Great Encyclopedic Dictionary (Bolshoy Entsyklopedicheskiy Slovar'). 1991. Moscow. Vol. 2. p. 623.

Great Encyclopedic Dictionary (Bolshoy Entsyklopedicheskiy Slovar'). 1997. St. Petersburg. p. 1338.

Great Soviet Encyclopaedia (Bolshaya Sovietskaya Entsyklopedia). 1934. Vol. 60.

Great Soviet Encyclopaedia (Bolshaya Sovietskaya Entsyklopedia). 1957.Vol. 47. pp. 6–7.

Grellmann, Heinrich. 1783. *Historischer Versuch über die Zigeuner*. Göttingen: Dietrich Verlag. English translation, 1807.

Gumilev, Leo. 1991. *Geography of Ethnos in the Historic Period*. St. Petersburg, and Moscow.

Gumilev, Leo. 1990. (originally 1978). *Ethnogenesis and the Biosphere of the Earth*. Private Leningrad.

Kalaydjieva, L., Gresham, D. and Calafell, F. 2004. 'Vlax Roma History: What Do Coalescent-based Methods Tell Us?' *European Journal of Human Genetics*, 12:285–92. (February)

Kalinin, V. 2005. *Mystery of the Baltic Roma*. Private. Minsk.

Kandyba, Viktor. 2002. *History of the Great Jewish Nation (Istoriya Drevnego Yevreyskogo Naroda)*. Private. St. Petersburg. p. 139.

Kenrick, D. 2004. *Gypsies: From the Ganges to the Thames*. Hatfield: University of Hertfordshire Press.

Lemon, Alaina. 2000. *Between Two Fires: Gypsy Performance and Romani Memory from Pushkin to Post-Socialism*. New York: Duke University Press.

Luby, S. *et al.*, eds. 1997. *Encyclopaedia Slovacika*. Bratislava.

Narbutt, Tadeusz. 1830. *The Historical Destiny of the Gypsy People (Rus: Historyczny Ludu Cyganskiego)*. Vilnius.

'On Reconciling Vagrant Gypsies to Labour', promulgated on 5 October 1957 by the Presidium of the Supreme Soviet, cited in D. M. Crowe, *A History of the Gypsies of Eastern Europe and Russia*. 1995. London: Palgrave, Macmillan. p. 188.

Prokhorov, A. *et al.*, eds. 1978. *Great Soviet Encyclopedia*. 3rd edition. Moscow. Vol. 28. pp. 607–8.

Russian Encyclopedic Dictionary (Russkiy Entsyklopedicheskiy Slovar'). 1873.Vol. 15.

Russian Encyclopedic Dictionary (Russkiy Entsyklopedicheskiy Slovar'). 1903.Vol. 75. pp. 304–30.

Schmidt, O. *et al.*, eds. 1934. *Great Soviet Encyclopaedia (Bolshaya Sovietskaya Entsyklopedia)*. Vol. 60. pp. 782–90.

Shapoval, V. 2007. *Manual for Self-tuition of the Gypsy Language*. Private. Moscow. p. 12.

Short Russian Encyclopedia. 2003. Moscow. Vol. R–YA. p. 707.

Skrypnyk, M. *et al.*, eds. 1959–65. *Ukrainian Soviet Encyclopedia (Ukrainskaya Sovietskaya Entsyklopedia)*. 1st edition. Lviv.

Slovakian Encyclopedia. 1977. Bratislava. Vol. I. pp. 320–2.

Smirnova-Seslavinskaya, Marijanna. June 2008. *The Cultural Essence of pro-Roma as a Binding Factor of Romani Ethnic Sub-Culture*, Paper delivered at the Romani International Conference, Kiev.

The paper also drew upon:

V. Kalinin correspondence with N. Bessonov.

V. Kalinin correspondence with V. Kovalenko.

V. Kalinin correspondence with V. Toropov.

V. Kalinin correspondence with M. Seslavinskaya/G. Tsvetkov.

V. Kalinin correspondence with T. Acton.

V. Kalinin correspondence with I. Makhotin.

V. Kalinin correspondence with M. Courtiade.

V. Kalinin correspondence with M. Bunto.

The possible implications of diasporic consciousness for Romani identity

Damian Le Bas
'Danes'

St John's College
Oxford University

'There is no greater sorrow on earth than the loss of one's native land.'
Euripides, 431 BCE

Euripides sees diaspora as most of us probably do: it is the spreading of people across lands and continents as seeds are spread on the wind. The place where these people come from is known to them and they probably mourn its loss. This is the expatriate's experience given a broader cultural voice. We can often see the fruits of it in writing, art and song. The feeling is all the more powerful when a common sense of exile unites *us*, when it is *our* native land that is lost, instead of merely 'one's'. Along these lines, the sociologist Richard Rorty has written:

> Our sense of solidarity is strongest when those with whom solidarity
> is expressed are thought as 'one of us', where 'us' means something
> smaller and more local than the human race. That is why 'because she
> is a human being' is a weak, unconvincing explanation of a generous
> action (1989: 191).

In relation to we Gypsies, use of the word 'diaspora', as of the attendant concepts of exile, dispossession and wandering, must be moderated by the fact that among many of us the notion of a far-flung homeland is either completely absent or very recent news. I speak only of my own people in the English puv[1].

My Uncle Georgie died in April this year at the age of 91, having no idea that his language or heritage was materially connected to India. However, land-focused conceptions of diaspora are the norm and have generated an enormous quantity of folk memory, literature and oral tradition that is increasingly influencing our self-understanding and that of Romanies around the world. Following initial puzzlement, I have started to explore these themes in my own poetry. Hermann Kesten, speaking of his exile, says, 'I wrote and wrote, so that I didn't have to cry'.

The Jewish diaspora is the most famed example of the scattering of a people. It is underpinned by the exile's feelings undergoing a process of formalisation, whence they are alchemically turned to solidarity and a cultural inheritance with persistent reference to the land of origin. As such, a brief historical overview of the Jewish diaspora is merited. This may help to clarify the variety of implications that diaspora might have for different ethnic/cultural groups, including Gypsies. I became obsessed with Jewish history and lore at university as it offered a precious lens through which to consider the analogous yet different situation of the Romani people.

Beginning from somewhere between 1200 and 800 BCE[2], a people connected by language, religious beliefs and ancestry lived in the area west of the river Jordan stated to stretch between the cities of Dan in the north and Beer-Sheba in the south. By the turn of the first millennium they were living under Roman military occupation in the Imperial province of Judaea. Although certain hierarchies, such as the priestly elite[3], remained, this was a clear instance of vassaldom and submission to an outside Empire.

It was no easy yoke to bear. Cycles of suppression, followed by revolt climaxed in colonial war. This led ultimately to the destruction of the Second Jewish Temple by the Roman Army in 70 CE and the exit of many Jews from the land. The key Jewish social continuities were shattered. Their religion, which was sacrificial and centred on Jerusalem, had lost with the destroyed temple its focal point, initiating the transition to Rabbinic Judaism and spelling the end of animal sacrifice. The old hierarchy of priests and rulers disappeared practically overnight and the ancient ties with Jerusalem went with them. The last stronghold of Jewish fighters and their families held out on Herod the Great's flat-peaked mountain fortress of the south, Masada, for two years before they chose suicide rather than enslavement to the Roman Army. The great holy city of Jerusalem was renamed Aelia Capitolina and transformed into a Roman military colony and horse-training centre. In Anglo-Romani we might call this the boryest ladge-up a foki could have kerred on 'em[4].

Although by this point some groups of Jews had already been living in diaspora communities for several centuries (such as the still extant community in Tehran, modern Iran) the cessation of these core features of Jewish religious and ethnic life had a massive impact. Many, if not most, Jews emigrated in search of a more tenable life. On the socio-religious side, study of the Bible became of paramount importance. Whole new bodies of text and commentary on it such as the Talmud themselves gained revered status and through this whole body of writing ran the memory of a people dispossessed. Here lies the key difference between the Jewish and Romani situations: the presence of precious ancient texts in which the roots of self-analysis can grow.

Euripides' words, written over 400 years before the beginning of the downfall of the Jewish land as Jewish, could almost have been written specifically about it. 'There is no greater sorrow on earth than the loss of one's native land', where this might mean the land which a people perceives as its crucible, even if its individuals have not been literally 'native' of it for a very long time[5].

The trouble with defining diaspora in terms of a single fixed geographical region as opposed to the fact of a people's scatteredness is that it has the potential to focus our attention on times and places that are not relevant to the experience of all particpiants in said disapora. Lemon asks 'if the original point of exile [is] the only place from which to define diaspora', and it is surely a question worth asking (2002: 42).

This transference of past to present experience can take various forms and I would suggest that these are not necessarily tied to the notion of lost homeland. In his essay on *Teaching Narratives of Exile*, Johannes Evelein refers to 'synchronic experiences lent a diachronic quality' (2002: 15) or experiences that happened at a particular point in time being invested with a significance for all times. This is a good entry point for understanding diaspora and the power it can have, even for those who live a very long time after its dust seems to have settled.

The key for understanding the implications this might have for Romani identity is relatively simple: in Romani history the 'synchronic experience', rather than being a punctual event or spark igniting a particular mode of self-understanding, has been a process lived as historical continuity. Exclusion and disenfranchisement from normal civil life or a combination of these have been persistent factors in the Gypsy experience. The complex interaction of hope, expectation and fear that these states may occur again reamins a persistent feature of Romani consciousness. This is unsurprising given the frequency and severity of the synchronic experiences, such as moving on, being moved on, being excluded from citizenship, or being murdered in their hundreds of thousands, that pepper the Romanies' history. That they should be lent a diachronic quality, a significance for the future as well as a rootedness in the past, is to be expected. Although not openly talked about, I believe such feelings lie close behind the tow-barred trucks, the axled homes and strong cob horses still proudly kept even by long-settled English Gypsies, and why they still prefer in most cases to call themselves 'Travellers'. We might not be moving right now, but we know we've got to be ready to do it at the drop of a hat.

It is also sufficient to rebut the popular and governmental slur that ceasing to be itinerant, whether temporarily or permanently, can rob an individual of Gypsy status. The short-termism, spite, opportunism and lack of perspective that underpin such a view are obvious. Furthermore, and as I have been building to, there has traditionally been no land of origin in which hopes for return or nostalgia for a past circumstance are invested. This is certainly a shifting and developing arena, as linguistic and ethnological research brings Romani links to India into further focus, but certainly until late modernity it has been difficult to imagine a coherent narrative of, say, repatriation *qua* Zionism being espoused by Gypsies, with India rather than Israel as its focus. It is perhaps the oral nature of Romani tradition that has resulted in the lack of a 'mythos' of the land of origin. Scholarly references are not necessary here, and I would instead direct the reader to attend the next Appleby horse fair and wander up and down Flashing Lane asking the Gypsies how Asian they feel. Among the typical barrage of talk about family, surnames, language, bender tents, hop fields, dukkerin', tin and nails, juks and Bedford lorries that I received as a Gypsy boy growing up in the 1980s, I never heard a single mention of the Gypsies' Indian roots. This is a situation in a definite state of flux, however[6], and links to India are increasingly on the radar of English Romani consciousness. This is no doubt due to another process highlighted as important by Evelein, 'Making ... curricula more responsive to societal needs ... the matching of the academic world with the "real" world' (2002: 17).

I mentioned above certain terms and concepts that are closely allied to that of diaspora and one of these is undoubtedly exile. Again, it is possible to open up the term from within the confines of its usual connotations of nationality. Shari Benstock, for example, has referred to the experience of women as exiles in male-dominated societies, expatriates in a 'terrain of patriarchy' (1989); Evelein also references the '*innere Emigration*' practised by dissenters living in Nazi Germany, an internal distancing from one's surroundings producing effects similar to those imposed by the concrete experience of exile. The feeling of exile, like diaspora, has an ephemerality of nature and malleability of meaning which allow it to influence the mindsets of individuals far removed from the material circumstances that first gave rise to it. As Benstock writes, 'The common denominator in the experience of metaphorical exile, then, is the existential sensation of difference, otherness, and our desire as human beings to retrace the path from the periphery back to our centre' (1989: 19).

All such talk of difference as sensation, though, must have as its converse differences which are objective. The persistence of a mother tongue can work as a catalyst on the experience of exile, or on the awareness that one is in some sense diasporic. Speaking a first language not spoken by the majority population points to a difference, to an origin somehow beyond local horizons, however foggy this origin might be. Language lends weight, significance and reality to sensations of difference. This is explored in the following stanza by the poet Czeslaw Milosz:

> But without you, who am I?
> Only a scholar in a distant country,
> a success, without fears and humiliations.
> Yes, who am I without you?
> Just a philosopher, like everyone else.
> *Czeslaw Milosz, 'My Faithful Mother Tongue', Collected Poems, 1931–87*

Milosz refers to the 'faithful mother tongue', and this fidelity is to be taken seriously. Language is one of the more functional heredities. It allows bridges with long-separated counterpart groups to be built. As such, it is susceptible to romanticisation but this does nothing to diminish the fact of its existence. The solidarity and security offered by language may be contrasted, however, with the fragility of the diasporic state when taken as a whole. Alaina Lemon speaks of 'the metaphysics of sedentarism', the accepted philosophy of majority (that is, here, settled) culture which continues to sneer at differing Romani conceptions of what constitutes a stable life (2002: 29–48). 'We often link representations of exile with images of marginality and loss, and contrast them with images of stable, authentic identity' (2002: 29). This is not to simplify a complex matter of relationships between communities, which includes the traditionally right-wing resentment of anyone who self-identifies as being part of a community within a state prior to proclaiming allegiance to that state. Such resentment is crystallised in John Wayne's outspoken sadness that anyone should want to be a 'hyphenated American', as though the designation 'American' were not good enough for them. To 'hyphenate' one's identity in a diasporic fashion is to spurn the 'gift' of nationality that will always be used as a fuel for the engine of xenophobia which drives on right-wing groups.

To continue with reference to language, it must be observed that in Romani studies this is by no means an unproblematic area. Certain clothed apes who have actually had academic qualifications conferred on them by European institutions are presently busy insisting that the Romani language has no reality as an extant, functional tongue. I can't speak for the rest of Europe, but if these people are right then mandi'a kakker rokker in Romanes ta-divvus 'cos the dinlo mushkras and bori-shero mollishers a kakker kom or jin the tatchipen what mandi's pukkerin.

That said (or not, if I didn't actually say it, as the case may be), a further problematic is that 'a Gypsy term is being usually accepted as genuine when an old Indian equivalent is found' (Pobozniak, 1964). I believe this is an oversimplification of what constitutes a language and agree with Thomas Acton that new words have and do acquire membership of the Romani lexicon over time. For example, Professor Acton correctly observes that the word 'brazen' is rarely used of a child outside the British Gypsy community, and when used by Travellers in conversation it often has a similar effect to the insertion of a well-chosen Romani word: an affirmation of the Gypsy identity of (at least some) of those present has occurred.

Interloper words are thought to ruin the 'purity' of the Romanies. This purity is important for outsiders when discussing the Gypsies in a way that it is certainly not for Gypsies ourselves. I think it is unlikely, however, that those who know no Gypsies themselves and little or nothing about our culture will hurry to lose their fetish for telling actual Gypsies that they don't fit the dilletante's preconstructed criteria. Perhaps such fetishes are best viewed as the harmless, if intellectually weightless, hobbies that they seem to me to be.

Crowley (1989: 77) wrote that, '[t]he English language, like the English people, is always ready to offer hospitality to all peaceful foreigners, words or human beings, that land or settle on her coasts'. English thereby manifests the 'qualities of liberality, decency or freedom' expected from its makers. It is notable that Romanes is not typically thought to be enriched by offering liberal hospitality to words that end up in its lexicon: instead, such words become evidence of the Gypsies' disintegrating cultural identity. The reader must judge for themselves whether the playing field is level in the way that languages are adjudged to be 'genuine' or 'polluted' with respect to the variegation of their lexical content. My instincts tell me that although Melvyn Bragg receives lavish praise for describing the wondrous mosaic of origins symbolised by modern English[7], one who takes the same attitude to a language such as Romanes is unlikely to gain even muted plaudits. 'For some, what is Indic replaces what is Romani: it is more Romani than Romani' (Lemon, 2002: 42). I have tried and failed to see the reasoning behind this sentiment-cum-perspective.

Katie Trumpener demonstrates that, in Western European literature, it is not that Gypsies actually store the old cultural forms, but that their appearances as characters in narratives, as 'rootless' marginals beyond civilisation's pale, triggers 'normal' narrative time to switch its flow into a suspended, timeless time. Trumpener argues that Gypsies evoke a dream of 'historylessness', and thus an 'idealizing envy of Gypsy life seemingly outside of history and beyond the reach of the authorities' (1992: 853). Anyone who thinks that modern English Romanies are beyond the reach of the authorities has never witnessed a police helicopter doing laps of the graveyard while their great-uncle is being buried by his sons and daughters.

The accusation given political voice by the apparently 'Honourable' Ann Widdecombe MP that modern English Gypsies have no more to do with the 'original' Romanies than Italians have to do with Julius Caesar is simply a crafty rephrasing of the older accusation that Gypsies used dye (often said to be walnut juice) to fake their appearance, since they couldn't possibly be a genuine people. Such accusations continue in the suspicion that surrounds people who identify themselves as Gypsies (and not just from the outside). 'But are you really,' the interrogator begins. The cyclic-oxymoronic situation is that the Gypsy speaking to you cannot be trusted to tell the truth, even about the fact that they are a Gypsy, yet the only reason for this lack of trust is *that they are a Gypsy*. I do hope such Kafkaesque ludicrousness becomes recognised for the inanity it is as soon as is humanly possible, as at present it remains a key component of many Gypsies' emerging diasporic experience, and it is boring and offensive.

This is possibly to be viewed as a side effect of diaspora, which for all peoples results in diversity of appearance where we presume things had once been clearer. Analogies with Jewish experience may be extended here. The tensions between Ashkenazi, Sephardi, Ethiopic (and recently Ugandan[8]) Jews in Israel are based at least in part on this 'anxiety of diversity' stemming from long centuries spent apart.

As we may or may not expect, diaspora is a concept which rests far more naturally and easily with Gypsies on the whole than it does with certain intellectuals. Lemon, again, provides us with a good example of this, and one which is heartening given the possibilities of anxiety outlined above:

> All manner of Romani women showed me family photographs in which they had dressed in saris, perhaps leaning against a Russian birch tree or the family car. Unlike Romani intellectuals, they did *not* speak of either Soviet cars or Russian words as un-Romani, as polluting an Indian essence; a car could converge with an Indian sari into an enviable image of Romani well being (2002: 43).

Taken to its conclusion, an overemphasis on Indo-centricity as a way of defining Gypsiness leads to thoughts along the following lines: 'The closer to India, the more Romani things are. Gypsy identity and purity would have been better served if the diaspora had never happened: the truest, *purest* Gypsies never left India in the first place, and the best of them certainly never got as far as speaking Romanes!'

This is why care must be taken over the nature and the extent of emphases on homogeneity, purity, and deep-*qua*-Indic language, as important as these may be to Romani communities themselves as persistent signifiers of identity. In various combinations they undoubtedly are. But, even if the thick end of the wedge may in practice never be reached, it should give us due cause to question the adequacy of the conceptions of diaspora that make such a conclusion possible. For there never lived an abstract Gypsy, a 'form' or 'archetype' according to Plato's or Jung's conception, at any point in history or in any corner of the world. We are a *people*, genuine and variegated. We are not factory-produced mannequins on conveyor belts that use a single pigment, or equip us with a single Indic tongue. The final, most crucial observation is that the absence of conveyor-belt Gypsies does not undermine our reality. It is the proof of it.

Notes

1   Romani, 'land'.

2   The quest to establish even an approximate date for the inception of Hebrew presence in the Western Levant has been a source of controversy since the mid–late nineteenth century. The efforts of early Biblical archaeologists such as William Foxwell Albright centred on the need they perceived to square the Old Testament narrative with the subterranean empirical reality. Although the 'Bible in one hand, spade in the other' approach has now been marginalised by mainstream enquiry, there is nothing like a scholarly consensus regarding the dates of early Israelite kingdoms, as Israel Finkelstein and Neil Asher Silberman's 2001 text *The Bible Unearthed* illustrates.

3   A hereditary class of temple administrators were charged with overseeing the proper conduct of sacrificial observance and festivals. These were the priests, of whom the High Priest had the greatest authority, both political and cultic. Caiaphas, who is portrayed in dubious light in the New Testament, was High Priest of the Second Temple.

4   Or, 'the most shameful circumstance that a people could be made to suffer'.

5   At this point my claim to any academic expertise ceases and the journeyman's thoughts begin. I speak as someone who has read only a small part of the wide literature of Romani studies, and as such I hope my thoughts may be helpful. However, I cannot guarantee their trustworthiness. So I will humbly emulate the likes of G. K. Chesterton, and, perhaps less auspiciously, Melvyn Bragg, in

begging to be admitted to the debate as a well-meaning amateur. I also entreat your forgiveness for any mistakes I make here. They will be exclusively and wholly mine.

6   I've heard more than one story about happy conversations springing up between British Asians and British Romanies when one of either group uses a word like 'pani' in open earshot.

7   See Melvyn Bragg, *The Adventure of English: the Biography of a Language*, Hodder and Stoughton, 2003.

8   A more complex issue, since Ugandan (Abuyudaya) Jews are known to be racially unrelated to other ethnic Jews, having embraced Jewish religion, culture and practice during the twentieth century.

References

Benstock, Shari. 1989. 'Expatriate Modernism: Writing on the Cultural Rim' in M. L. Broe, ed., *Women's writing in Exile*. North Carolina: Chapel Hill University Press. pp. 19–40.

Crowley, A. 1989. *The Confessions of Aleister Crowley, An Autohagiography.* London: Penguin Arkana.

Evelein, Johannes F. 2002. 'Ethics, Consciousness and the Potentialities of Literature: Teaching Narratives of Exile' in D. Radulescu; ed., *Realms of Exile.* Oxford: Lexington Press. pp. 15–28.

Lemon, Alaina. 2002. 'Telling Gypsy Exile: Pushkin, India and Romani Diaspora' in D. Radulescu, ed., *Realms of Exile.* Oxford: Lexington Press. pp. 29–48.

Pobozniak, T. 1964. *A Grammar of the Lovari Dialect.* Krakow: Polska Akademia Nauk.

Rorty, Richard. 1989. *Contingency, Irony and Solidarity.* Cambridge: Cambridge University Press.

Trumpener, Katie. 1992. 'The Time of the Gypsies: A People Without History'. *Critical Inquiry* 18(4): 843–84.

6

The importance of the Romany and Traveller Family History Society (RTFHS)

Janet Keet-Black

Founder, Editor and Secretary, RTFHS

Family history is one of those areas that for many years so-called serious researchers and academics, with one or two notable exceptions, have considered to be somewhat amateur and therefore of little merit.

Twenty years ago, on the death of an uncle, it occurred to me that all the old folk were going and taking so much knowledge with them. It became important to me to find out as much as I could about my own history, thinking at the time that there would be little in the way of documented evidence for me to find and that it was unlikely there would be anyone else out there undertaking similar work.

However, although there were very few researching their Gypsy ancestry 20 years ago, those of us who were so involved eventually made contact and it soon became apparent that it would be useful to pool our knowledge and any resources we might have collected.

The Romany and Traveller Family History Society (henceforth RTFHS) was founded in 1994 in Chailey, Sussex with an inaugural meeting of six family historians. Membership now approaches 700. The aim of the society is not to follow the road back 1,000 years but to learn and record our personal histories within the context of British history. Genealogy is about names and dates, and forms only part of the research process. It is written into the RTFHS constitution that:

> The object of the society shall be to advance the education of the public in the study of family history and social history ... [and] collect, publish, co-ordinate and make accessible any documents

and records, including oral records, particularly relating to Gypsies, travelling showmen, and other itinerants ... [and to] promote the presentation of such documents and records.

RTFHS members undertake original research and are advised to use already published material as no more than pointers to the past – it is up to the individual to prove as correct anything that has been previously recorded. The advice is simple: back everything up with documented evidence.

We dive into archives that perhaps have not seen the light of day for a century or two. In such a way, a founder member discovered an early seventeenth-century word list containing Romani words that the RTFHS was able to bring to the wider world in the form of a published booklet. Such results make Gypsy family history research legitimate. We are amateurs only in the sense that we work without payment or funding. Indeed, we can often validate or discredit previously published research.

To take as an example plurality of baptism, whereby a Gypsy couple had a child baptised more than once. Although this practice had been touched upon, I first came across an example of it when trawling archives in East Sussex Record Office. When travelling through Sussex, a couple had a child baptised five times on five consecutive days. Since that first sighting, this couple has been tracked the length and breadth of England and Wales and, over a period of ten years, between 1830 and 1840, they have appeared in baptismal registers over 300 times. The search is ongoing.

Sometimes, however, academics and Gypsiologists are incorrect in their assumptions. It was suggested in correspondence by Thomas Acton that Gypsies did not use the term 'Traveller' as a self-ascription until the early 1900s but RTFHS members showed Gypsies were described as such in parish registers from as early as the 1600s, although so too were indigenous travellers and others who may have been passing through the area on business. It would appear to be the generic term used by the parish incumbent to describe anyone who was travelling through the area.

There is documented evidence that as a self-ascription it was a term used by Gypsies long before the 1900s: in a newspaper report of the 1860s, Keziah Lee was quoted as saying, 'My name is Keziah Lee. I am a Traveller.'

Similarly, it has been written that the first real attempt to found a school specifically for Gypsy children was in Surrey in the 1900s but some of us were already aware of the Farnham Gypsy Asylum and Industrial School that was founded in the 1840s in Farnham, Dorset, thanks to that wonderful, largely untapped source, the oral tradition that prompts the visits to records offices and the National Archive at Kew. My great-great-grandfather was a pupil there.

We now know the identity of the unnamed Gypsies written about in Queen Victoria's diaries and featured in her watercolours. We know who they are, have given them names, written about them and can produce the documents to back it all up.

And in response to those who curl their lips in contempt and say, 'Gypsies didn't go to war, they all dressed as women or ran off to Ireland,' we can say, 'Here are the medal rolls, the Victoria Cross, the DCM, the Military Medals – and here are the photographs and names of the Gypsies commemorated on war memorials alongside other sons, fathers and brothers.'

Family history research is as valid as any other and the wealth of information and knowledge acquired over the past 20 or so years is impressive, if sometimes overlooked by some amongst the so-called erudite scholars. With this ongoing research comes the sense that we are reclaiming our history, and although it is not an RTFHS initiative – not everyone is comfortable with the idea – a member of the Lock family has set up a Romani DNA project in the search for answers to the question of our origins.

In addition to this sense of owning our own history, one of the unexpected but encouragingly positive outcomes of RTFHS membership has been the slow breaking down of barriers. Many Travellers were – and some still are – suspicious of the family historian, and although there is still a long way to go, family researchers are now being invited onto sites and into the homes of their newly found distant Traveller cousins. In visiting those homes, the researcher who has discovered a Gypsy great-great-grandfather and taken to the romantic notion that he was 'a pure-blooded Romani, not like the Travellers today', and profess immense pride – in other words, not at the bottom of my garden but yes please on my tree – suddenly discovers that their hosts aren't really so different from themselves.

Conversely, Cathay Birch, an RTFHS member who lives on a site, wrote:

I just wish I had known about you fifteen years ago. Joe, my husband and I retain and live the Romany life amongst Romanies and when we go outside the group, so to speak, the persecution we have suffered and non-acceptance has been heartbreaking. My husband is a pastor and we keep within the law and don't cause trouble but that's made no difference – but in joining the Society we have found so many friends and people that will invite us into their homes and come and visit us in our home. We feel we are totally accepted and even though many of you don't now live as Travellers you are interested in us and you have treated us as equals and we feel we love and would be pleased to see any one of you. It's so refreshing to be amongst friends rather than confined, although often on the road, to a few other Roms, who of course we love, but we have now widened our vision and our friendships.

Another member who, having been brought up with the knowledge of her ethnicity but encouraged to remain silent for fear of prejudice, wrote, 'I for one wholeheartedly enjoy this group – for the first time in my life I feel free to comment as I wish and to be myself. It has enabled me to openly declare what I am and be proud of it'.

Then there is the discovery of a parent born in a tent, or 'under the hedge', and the sense of relief that comes with it. The whispers, the exchanged looks, the family secret that had been locked away, and the niggling feeling that you are somehow different but you don't know why, are all explained.

Unfortunately, in some ways the Romany and Traveller Family History Society has become a victim of its own success. Freelance writers have jumped on the family history bandwagon and command fees for writing on the subject of Gypsy family history, even though they may have no Gypsy ancestry themselves and have to draw on the findings and published works of RTFHS members. Seldom is one of our members approached to write an article or offered payment for doing so.

To facilitate family history research, some RTFHS members have set up their own websites and information that might once have come to the society is appearing online. Although this may make it accessible to larger numbers of researchers, paradoxically it excludes many whom for one reason or another do not have access to the Internet.

The concern now is what will happen when websites are taken down. What will happen in the long term to the wealth of information being held by so many individuals? The ideal solution would be to preserve it all in a central repository, but the universities that currently hold Gypsy archives cannot accept more.

There have been murmurings of a Romani archive for the UK similar to that set up by Ian Hancock in the US. We certainly need one in the UK, not necessarily in a university but one that is properly funded and somewhere that Travellers can feel comfortable visiting. Somewhere that they, and we, can say that at last we have an acknowledged place in British history. We didn't just drop out of space and land behind a hedgerow; we've been here over 500 years.

7

The RTFHS: a special family history society

Michael Wayne Jones

I am 49. I discovered that I had Romani Gypsy ancestry just four years ago. Growing up as an only child in the 60s and 70s in a relatively sheltered rural community in west Wales meant that I remained unaware of many things that were realities of life for the average child from the towns, cities and suburbs of Britain, or indeed for a child from an average travelling family still on the road at that time. Looking back, mine was an idyllic childhood, purely working class, with loving, hardworking parents and a supportive extended family.

But discussion about family history simply did not take place. Not because no one *wanted* to discuss it – it never occurred to us to be interested in it. For the working class, life was hard and my parents' main concern was to get by financially, to survive just above the breadline, and to give me an education and a good start in life that they did not benefit from themselves. We had no time or inclination to ponder or reflect on just who our ancestors may or may not have been! We lived our lives without enquiring – it simply didn't occur to us. I do not believe that I am alone in becoming more curious much later in life.

The loss of my father, who died prematurely at 47 when I was a teenager of 16, was, as you might expect, traumatic for my mother and I. We coped as best we could. So we came through and got on with our lives. It was not until many years later that I became interested in genealogy and tracing the family tree.

A very happy marriage with a wonderful wife, a decent career, and football playing and management (albeit at amateur level) took up all my time in the intervening years – not to mention the business of enjoying life. Thinking about it now, although it did not seem to bother me or preoccupy me at the time, I did feel different growing up, not just by being an only child, but deep down, there was a difference which I could not put my finger on.

It occurred to me some four or five years ago that, despite all this relative success, there was something missing. Who was I? I had no real idea. How did I get here? What was my ethnic background? Funnily enough, I had always wondered about the fact that I am olive skinned. I was always darker than my school friends. I recall that my father, his father and I all turned even darker after a very short period in the sun! Not that skin hue is necessarily a pointer towards Gypsy ancestry, of course. But it was a clue. In addition, I have blood group B Rh+, a blood type owned by apparently just 8 per cent of the population of Great Britain. That also made me wonder even more.

My granddad, who died within three weeks of my father, was adept at tap-dancing and what I now know of as step-dancing. He played the spoons, and granny the harmonica. I didn't twig – thinking they were just musically talented. We lived in a house, so there was no obvious indicator there either. No one ever mentioned Gypsy or Traveller connections – none of my aunts or uncles or older cousins ever spoke of it, at least not to me. Even today, I can glean nothing from them. They won't open up. So with no one to ask and left to my own devices, I set out to trace my family history in 2005, making sure to respect their wishes and a sure need for anonymity. I knew I was half 'Welsh' and half 'English', my father being born and bred in Wales and my mother from London originally. But that was all I knew.

I did what all beginners do, fumbled around, read some books, bought the magazines, took advice, searched the web, interrogated the censuses and finally, ordered certificates. They were the first sign that things were beginning to unravel, when, in 2006, I found some family certificates that showed birth in tents and caravans, occupations such as hawker, travelling hawker, tinsmith, basket maker and others. Marriage certificates provided extra clues about occupations and, for example, illiteracy.

Then I discovered the Romany and Traveller Family History Society. Unique in its field, the RTFHS's coverage is national and international, not confined to county-based research and information exchange. This is necessary because of the nomadic nature of the Romani people. Our ancestors travelled around and their descendants are to be found in all corners of the country and indeed swathes of the globe. The society helped me to make sense of what I was finding and to learn about other people's experiences of discovering their family tree. I was struck by how familiar my experience of not knowing was to other members. This has often been the case in the past when the travelling life has been left behind; families were housed in local authority housing and the culture and background were spoken of no more. I believe this was done to protect the children from discrimination that their parents and all the previous generations undoubtedly suffered.

To my mind, the value of the RTFHS cannot be overstated. The membership is currently around the 650 mark and the officers are highly knowledgeable and experienced, forming a dedicated and hardworking committee whose aim is to help others to learn, develop their knowledge of research methods and ultimately their family roots. Without the society, I would not have come this far over the last three years. They are helping me with my journey of discovery, which will continue for the rest of my life, I expect. It is now a passion with me — an addiction. My focus has become the Welsh Romani families and Welsh families of Irish Traveller extraction, all kinsfolk of my own paternal grandparents.

In addition to the experience shared by the RTFHS, publications of real note that have helped me with my research in this niche area have been the following:

- *My Ancestors Were Gypsies* by Sharon Floate, a leading official of the RTFHS.
- Various works by the renowned modern-day expert and Gypsiologist Robert Dawson.
- The RTFHS Journal *Romany Routes.*
- *The Welsh Gypsies: Children of Abram Wood* by Eldra Jarman.
- The *Journal of the Gypsy Lore Society* — a rich genealogical source from the 1880s to the present day that no true Gypsy family historian should ignore.

So on I continue with my journey, finding out more about not only my direct ancestors and the wider family, but all the Welsh families, all of whom in some shape or form descend from the father of all of the Welsh Romanies Abram Wood, 1699–1799. I can trace my ancestry back to Abram through his granddaughter Alabaina Jones (nee Wood). I cannot say how immensely proud I am of that fact.

Above all, I now know who I am, and that is attributable in no small part to the RTFHS.

Afterword: Rom, Roma, Romani, Kale, Gypsies, Travellers, and Sinti … pick a name and stick with it, already!

Gregor Dufunia Kwiek

My final comments as the chair of the *All Change* conference related to an event that took place early in 2008, when a group of young Roma gathered to discuss the problems we face as Roma in Sweden, and how we could overcome them. It is the purpose of this paper to express the thinking behind the remarks I made in closing this conference.

The young Roma at the meeting in Sweden came from various backgrounds. They related their personal achievements, some stating that they had achieved success by concealing their Romani identity, while others explained that they used their identity to succeed in what is known as the *Gypsy Industry*. The topic of discussion at this meeting was how to gain positions of power, the better to influence social conditions for Roma in Sweden. My view was that we need to have people in sectors such as media, health, law and politics, not as Roma but as citizens of the state, and at the same time we need to be organised and to act as a unified body whenever we as a people are denied our rights because we are Roma. I emphasised this by pointing out how that same year commuters had become dependent upon taxi drivers when bus drivers went on strike. A good portion of taxi drivers in Sweden have an Arabic or Iranian ethnic background. Some had been doctors, lawyers and teachers in their countries of origin. I used this example to point out that education does not promise positions of power, but finding yourself in a role that makes others dependent on you can give you leverage to achieve a desired outcome.

Many of the Roma at the meeting expressed the view that we are disorganised and lack structures for unification. One example was mother-tongue instruction where students not only have different *dialects*, but different *familylects* and *idiolects* that make the classes difficult to carry out. It was at this point that I explained why I am not in favour of unification.

In Sweden, researchers have divided the various Romani groups according to when they originally migrated to Sweden, which in turn has become the paradigm for group representation. This has led to the creation of organisations and projects that try to be as representative as possible of the constructed classification. The problem, however, has been that at times the groups differ so much in their values, traditions and interests that it has been difficult to find common ground. The problem with self-identification has been that some groups have seen language as the instrument that identifies them as Roma: for others it has been the focus on customs and traditions, while in some cases physical appearance is seen as the prime identifier. Furthermore, some groups consider *all* these factors to be constitutive of identity while others may not regard *any* as being particularly important.

General frameworks that could unite Roma at the EU level have been developed in areas such as mother-tongue instruction. One such framework is entitled *The Curriculum Framework for Romani*. This framework has general outlines on how to evaluate mother-tongue instruction for Romani children, making suggestions for course subjects, and continuously making the point that *Romanipe* should be included in the instruction but without a definition of what *Romanipe* is. The idea behind this is that different groups will automatically implement their own correct concepts of *Romanipe*. The problem here resides in the fact that no nation or people has a single, consistent ideology that binds them. For example, in the education systems of some western countries, class and religion have been excluded as discriminatory. Some nations, on the other hand, have simply used their country's dominant religion as the binding structure of their education system: since the Roma do not have a dominant religion that can unify them, this option would be difficult to implement. The idea that *Romanipe* can unify the Roma would be the equivalent of saying that the love of nature is what unifies Swedish society. The reality is that not all Swedes are fond of nature, and see their *Swedishness* as far more complex, notwithstanding the fact that differences in age, religious background, political affiliation, social and regional background will all contribute to different personal understandings of what it means to be Swedish.

Visiting Vilnius, Lithuania, I had gone to the consulate to arrange documents. While waiting to be called to the window I had nothing to do and began reading some pamphlets about Sweden. It was interesting that the pamphlets did not refer to the love of nature or common traditional rituals such as Midsummer as a means of describing Swedish identity, but rather located its strengths in democratic values and attitudes to gender equality. It was at this point that I began considering how funding motivates us to try and implement structures that would not work for a Swedish society that is not homogeneous, let alone for the Romani people who do not have a standardised language, a powerful media that can communicate common values, or a plot of land that could be the site of a national monument.

The meeting I have referred to did not come about by chance. It was arranged because an academic Romani reference group, the proceedings of which were approved for citation in governmental and academic documents, was under development. All those involved in the reference group agreed that it would be important for us Roma to engage in it as it would give us the opportunity to express our views when it came to Romani culture as an academic subject. It would also give us the chance to question why Romani studies remains primarily the province of non-Romani scholars. Why could this situation not be reversed? Why could we not have non-Romani reference groups that were specialists in health, politics and law in case we were not, and use them as a reference? These were the kinds of questions that were posed at the meeting.

As these issues arose at the meeting, the discussion turned to the *Gypsy Industry*. People related how non-Romani organisations had sought to combat *antiziganism* by having a 'token Gypsy' at their conference whether they were qualified or not. We were all familiar with the idea of how the *Gypsy Industry* was made up of non-Roma who then selected Roma to join them so they could claim 'joint effort'. We also discussed how some non-Romanis claimed Romani heritage in order to build a career within a sector such as academia. I had met just such a person who claimed to have Romani heritage. This person wrote a book about some of his experiences. One of the most interesting sections in the book included remarks about people who were my relatives. I contacted those relatives and told them I had come across this person, and that was when I learned that the author was not Romani at all, but was someone who merely worked with them and who had learned their language from them. Indeed, something similar took place in Sweden during the 1970s when a man claimed to be Romani, following contact with a Romani community and, because he was educated, he proposed to act as a spokesperson for the community. However, this did not happen as the community were opposed to the idea and preferred self-representation, even where the tools of education were lacking.

Of course there are some people who have learned about their Romani heritage later in life and who then seek to engage with the community. Indeed I have some second cousins who did not know they were Romani and only learned of their origins as adults. Similarly, I have a great-great grandmother who is of non-Romani origin, but I can hardly identify myself as being non-Romani. My point here is that the issue of identity is a complex one. The cousins I mentioned had a grandfather who left the community, married a non-Romani woman and taught his children about their Romani background in a negative manner. His grandchildren learned later about their background and contacted me via the internet. They did not join the community of course, but still wanted to learn about our history, culture and language. In another case, a young woman was raised by a non-Romani parent in Poland before finding her father in Stockholm. By the time she reached her forties she had settled in Stockholm, her children have married local Roma, and she is now a member of the Romani community in Stockholm. Another woman grew up hiding her identity for most of her life: she has now become an activist, and teaches psychology at the Police Academy.

Thus the discussion brought up two issues that revolved around the *Gypsy Industry*. One was concerned with how non-Romani institutions claim collaboration with the Romani community by including the participation of a *token Gypsy*. The other regarded how non-Romani people construct a false Romani identity to gain a foothold in the *Gypsy Industry*. At the *All Change* conference, Michael Wayne Jones explained how he had learned about his Romani origins via the *Romany and Traveller Family History Society*, and in my final comments at the conference I relayed what it was that bonded this man's story to my own. The history of racial and discriminatory violence against Roma, Gypsies and Travellers has imposed limitations on our knowledge about our origins. As a young man, the history of my own people was unknown to me until I came across Dr Ian Hancock's book *The Pariah Syndrome*. It was through this book that I began to pass on knowledge of our history to other members of the community. The arguments that I heard in response from many of these Roma are represented in my poem, *I am the Common Rom* (see page v). What binds us is not *Romanipe* in itself, but the very racism and discrimination which distance us from it!

I mentioned above an observation that was made at the meeting in Sweden, about gaining leverage. This must be achieved by finding a means of inclusion rather than exclusion, which would mean not using *Romanipe* or language as its driving force. Rather, it would mean changing the *Gypsy Industry* into a *Romani Industry*, controlled by Romani people. Access to the community, knowledge of it, and bridge-building between non-Romani and Romani society are key elements, without which efforts such as the EU Decade of Roma Inclusion will have little effect. Problems are escalating and the *Gypsy Industry* cannot deal with them because it lacks the ability to actually reach the community. The point made here is not an ideological one but a pragmatic one, and it is through discussion of pragmatics that we will be able to address why many Roma hide their identity, and how this problem can be tackled.

Naturally, if non-Roma continually represent us, as individuals and institutions, there will be little opportunity for any coming out of the closet to take place, so to speak. By being explicit about the fact that the *Gypsy Industry* only leads to endless conference topics, while the actual Roma go on hiding their identity and surviving by the few means available to them, the nature of this Catch 22 situation becomes clear. After all, in order for Roma to openly admit who and what they are, the channels of communication must be made available *to* them and not simply be *about* them or be imposed *upon* them.

Greater Romani visibility acts like a lighthouse directing ships in the sea. Romani-run institutions like the *Romany and Traveller Family History Society* act as lighthouses. Most certainly, one can find counter-arguments to the points I make in this paper, and perhaps I am not placing enough concern on individuality. However, I must point out that this paper concentrates its efforts on socio-ethnic groups rather than individual concerns. In other words, in this paper I have argued that the cohesive means which have been used to try to unify individuals who are Romani have been dysfunctional. I am also pointing out that it is the organic effects of racism and discrimination which unify us: we are all robbed in some shape or form of our identity as a people. By accepting the idea that we are different, we become pragmatic and deal with problems with weaponry that can fight it, rather than simplistic and false notions about what unites us (language, tradition, ideology, etc). Such notions are bound to lead us to bicker in attempting to identify what is Romani and what is not.

LIVERPOOL
UNIVERSITY PRESS

Romani Studies

EDITOR: YARON MATRAS, UNIVERSITY OF MANCHESTER

Romani Studies is an international, interdisciplinary journal publishing modern scholarship in all branches of Romani/Gypsy studies. Under the sponsorship of the Gypsy Lore Society (formerly Gypsy Lore Society, North American Chapter), *Romani Studies* features articles on the cultures of groups traditionally known as Gypsies as well as Travellers and other peripatetic groups. These groups include, among others, those referring to themselves as Rom, Roma, Romanichels, Sinti and Travellers. The journal publishes articles in history, anthropology, sociology, linguistics, art, literature, folklore and music, as well as reviews of books and audiovisual materials.

2 issues per year
Institutions: £45.00 / $80.00
ISSN: 1528-0748

To subscribe to *Romani Studies*:

Email: subscriptions@marston.co.uk
Telephone Marston Book Services on +44 [0]1235 465 537
Or visit the journal website: www.romanistudies.org

www.liverpool-unipress.co.uk